734293 14.50
16F1

E DUE

AUG 8 1985
MAY 2 4 1987
NOV 18 1987

Cat. No. 23-221

WE DIE BEFORE
WE LIVE

Daniel Berrigan

WE DIE BEFORE WE LIVE
Talking With the Very Ill

THE SEABURY PRESS, NEW YORK

1980
The Seabury Press
815 Second Avenue
New York, N.Y. 10017

Library of Congress Cataloging in Publication Data
Berrigan, Daniel.
We die before we live.
1. Death. 2. Terminal care—Moral and religious
aspects. 3. St. Rose's Home. 4. Berrigan Daniel.
5. Catholic Church—Clergy—Biography. 6. Clergy—
United States—Biography. I. Title.
BT825.B455   362.1'96029   80-16835   ISBN 0-8164-0462-3

To everyone at St. Rose's
In awe and admiration

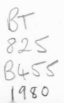

CONTENTS

WHERE DEATH ABOUNDED, LIFE
St. Rose's Home

I first heard of St. Rose's three years ago, from a friend who had begun working there as an orderly. I was in the usual spinning orbit of teaching, writing, and pilgrimaging to the Pentagon to throw ashes and blood at the idols. Something was lacking; whether true ikons, physical work, or self-testing. I phoned the sister in charge. Could I hire out as a part-time volunteer?

What ensued I like to call, in a modest way, history. I am by no means capable or willing to tell all, nor is there need to. Rather speedily, and in a wonderfully offhand way, I was given a tour of the place; my questions were answered sensibly; it was made clear that if I wished to help I would be welcome.

It gave to ponder, as the French say. Here was a spanking facility humming with compassion and energy, up to the minute in equipment; to it the urban poor came to die; within it the intangible realities of life ("the things which are unseen") were available, abundant. Here, moreover, sisters and orderlies underwent, orchestrated, that Great Day which the spirituals said was "gonna be."

All this struck my earth-bound mind. And there was more, as I was to learn. In payment for such care, such friendship, no money crossed the palm. No guest paid, no one could pay. It was a rule of the order, strictly adhered to. It struck me: here we had a stunning instance of the ethical cemented into natural law. The rule was all but metaphysical: no money. No insurance; no red, white, or blue crosses; no bread from city, state, feds. No payment from any patient or relative, no matter how highly or mightily placed, or how lowly.

I spell out the rule in some detail to show how it spun about in my mind, dazzling. Who could have believed it? It had, I thought, the delicious evanescent aura of the more than human. Then I pondered the phrase "more than human." What in the world could be more than human? The more I pondered, the clearer it became; the phrase meant "simply human." Which is not to deny that the hospital came as a salutary assault on my lowered expectations.

How marred our hopes are! Things which should be available to all inevitably cost a great deal. The few things which are still free of price tags are polluted: air, parks, vistas.

But in any sane scheme of things, that almost unimaginable world that shone on our retinas like a mirage, like the kingdom of God, would not good medical care be free to all?

We were so used to paying up; a cross of gold, as the old orators used to intone; the degradation of the buck, fast or slow, inflated or sound, lies heavy on us. Goods and services became bads and disservices; before the eyes of the poor, they dangle out of reach; and for the rest of us, who desperately tread dark waters, such things are overpriced, begrudged, performed in bad spirit, left to others. What profession today ministers to essential needs, lives up to its own ideals?

Here and there, parochial schools in New York City hold the line. They still do what they once set out to do: serve the poor, teach the children of the poor. Nuns live in the ghetto, poor, standing by. All reports, including secular ones, say the instruction is sound, the children are making it.

Hospitals have fared less well, for a multitude of reasons. The cost of medical care, as is no news to anyone, has soared out of sight. Nineteenth-century orders of women, founded to do basic medical work among the immigrants and poor, have withered before the blight of the buck. Either the (male) diocesan chanceries have grabbed the facilities and "integrated" them into church-state hyphens, or the sisters have given in, done the same sad thing on their own. In either case, the mirage of bigger and better has won over the solid reality of small and beautiful. By now the Catholic hospitals, in any given town, including New York, are a crawling sprawl, big and getting bigger, pledged to roughly the same medical practices, abortion excepted, as their secular counterparts.

In the process, original intentions have all but vanished. Where nuns are present in the typical hospital, they are more apt to be commandeering switchboards or accounts offices than nursing the sick and dying. The services are secularized, with all the ambiguity that implies; so, it goes without saying, are the finances. The poor receive the kind of health care which the state allows or disallows, another function of that bulldozing of existence euphemistically, and despite all malpractice, named "welfare."

St. Rose's Home, for reasons both complex and fascinating, has escaped such attrition. Let me avoid meandering, and simply report that this unique hospital for the dying has hewn to its original line, literally and consistently. The sisters do today what their founder set out to do some ninety years ago; an achievement that strikes one, in the American farce of size, quantity, media puffing, death and

dying chic, the stalling of much originality and imagination
in the stuck culture—strikes one as either a triumph of plain
stubborn vision, or of specially tender providence, or both.

You don't have to be poor in America to die badly. You
just have to be dying; the rest is supplied. And by "dying
badly," I don't refer to immediate physical care, on which,
bad or good, the rich have the usual monopoly.

Let me speak of the obverse, "dying well," as St. Rose's
has helped me understand the term. Dying well implies a
sense of one's self, a hand on the rudder, a mind that despite
rip tides and near swamping is reasonably able to give and
take, to read signals and send them out; for the conscious
duration, those who die well hold a sense both of anguish
and humor, as well as a sense of their plight, discomfort,
degree of pain, etc. Such hardy spirits turn the tables, show
a good face to others, including family, friends, etc. I recol-
lect the old idea that there is an art of dying, as there is an
art of living. And I suspect that the two are more closely
joined than is commonly admitted.

Let us take matters further. St. Rose's is a hospital for the
dying; but not just for any dying. It is a hospital for those
dying of cancer. The dying are, moreover, poor; indeed,
poverty is a chief criterion for admission; by presumption,
the rich can choose to go elsewhere, and pay as they go.

Such arrangements color the atmosphere of St. Rose's,
give the place a special quality, precious to Christian under-
standing. Let me speak for myself. I belong to an order
whose first ideal has been all but obliterated in America
(though I am delighted to report that elsewhere, among
poor nations and peoples, its spirit flourishes and its tribe
increases). Here, the likes of me fight such unlikely battles
as, e.g., trying to persuade one of our large universities to
disclaim the blood money of the unlamented shah of Iran.

And, need I add, I lose the skirmish. Yoked to such bloody helpmeets do we die, in harness to the culture.

With what a sense of refreshment, self-restoring, I came to St. Rose's. Slowly I sensed that an atrophied sixth or seventh sense was coming to life; a sense of recognition. I was awakening to the lineaments of the Catholic; that face which, like the face of Christ, is hideously worked over in America, rendered nearly unrecognizable by a thousand clumsy or malicious hands, our own. Where could one turn in the great city, like the blind, and with the tips of one's fingers touch that face of grandeur, of inner light, wordless, the face of advocate, friend?

I am clumsily shuffling words which the poor and dying have repeated to me, with insistent fervor, a hundred times. What a good place St. Rose's is! Jew and gentile, old and young, streetwise, moneywise, prisonwise—the chorus is remarkable. It converges, in fact, on what the old theology texts used to call an irrefragable argument for the truth. We are in presence of what seems elsewhere, and in many exalted places, to be simply an absence; I mean the church. Hence the shock of recognition; what Chesterton used to call, in despair over language and its shortcomings, simply "the Thing."

Colorless as water, cool rather than perfervid, subtle rather than evangelistic, veiled as befits mystery, skilled in the thousand ways of conveying love, undeclarative, able to hold and let go, smiling and weeping, modest as befits the human condition in extremis. . .

Dying well, I have suggested, implies dying as one has lived; so does dying badly. One finds that, with a little help, the poor die well. This is an unremarkable observation to anyone who knows the poor; I want to reflect on this.

One begins at the hospital by being silent, observing

things. Patients come to us, for the large part, from the lower-income levels of the city. They are the people whom I see on the subway and bus en route to the hospital: the working poor. Now and again, we greet a different guest of the days of the tolling bell—a kind of sub-subway person, a prisoner, an addict, alcoholic, a classic outsider, outside the economy, outside the social contract. In either case, poor or outcast, the people we serve have only the most tenuous handhold on America. They have lived and are about to die at the edge of almost everything that constitutes the Dream: money, profession, opportunity, the upward escalator.

With regard to working people, this fact implies an irony. By and large, their working lives offered true benefits; they were maintenance people, transit workers, supers in apartment buildings, printers, seamen, short order cooks, postal workers, police. As in every great city of the world, they rode the subways in the early morning to, from, long days and nights of labor. Their rhythms, their faces and bodies, especially their hands, remind me vividly of the description of the early morning street scene in Silone's *Bread and Wine*. Spina, the marxist mystic disguised as a priest, walks about Rome:

> . . . Workmen came trooping along from every side, and there was a beauty in the air that moved Spina deeply, the marvelous beauty of Rome at dawn, when there is no one in the streets but honest people going to work, walking quickly and talking little. . .

Later the scene changes:

> [Spina] went down the Via della Navicella and the Via Claudia toward the center of the city, in order to see it once more. But the beauty of Rome had faded. The workers had disappeared from the streets, and no one was to be seen now but men in

uniform, government clerks, priests, and nuns going shopping. Rome was now a different place.

Later in the morning, the scene is startlingly different:

> And between ten and eleven, when the big parasites began to appear, the hierarchs, the higher officials of the ministries, and the monsignori with their violet stockings, Rome suddenly became odious in his sight. . .

As to our patients, one could not, I think, claim that their slender stake in the Dream had begotten an inspired social or political sense. Hardly. Still, one notices time and again that a life of near poverty, lived close to the bone, a life of relative insecurity, one moreover whose sense of dignity was built on worthwhile work—all this helps one say a good amen at the approach of bell, book, and candle. The moorings that bind these lives to the mainland have never been that firm; now they are slipped with ease. There is detachment in the air, good humor, even a sense of celebration at times. Folks josh one another, look out for one another; some want to be wheeled about the wards to greet those who are stuck in bed. Up to the final letting go, the prelude is not depression or damp; it is sunny, warm of will.

To grasp something of this, one has to go beyond therapeutic convention. Even if the staff saw the hospital as a kind of mini-*Titanic* heading toward catastrophe (and they do not), it still must be reported that there are no "social facilitators" aboard. People are employed or volunteer, not to daub a presentable cosmetic on the hard face of death, or to whoop things up despite all. We are there to help make life bearable, to make some sense of it, make it attractive as long as it lasts—together. There is respect for privacy, respect for moods and imbalances, a spoiling attention to diet, from kosher to Tipperary Irish. There is an unobtrusive religious feel about the place, which now and again surfaces in sacrament or prayer or plain talk about death; but only on the initiative of the patients. No one is force-fed, whether on religion, psychosemantics or -antics. Little account is taken, except where suffering or depression require, as to being in or out of purported stages of dying. Things are reasonably lively, sometimes even rambunctious.

There are, moreover, no psychiatrists or social workers on the premises. This information is conveyed here as a mere report; I have never had the impression that such skills are subjects of prejudice. The hospital is simply in another stream. It operates on the principle that work with the dying, though hair-raisingly difficult at times, can be done well by normally endowed people with the heart for it, that the work can be done on a rather modest budget, that ingenuity and inventiveness are the handmaids of skill and will flourish given the chance.

There is a second principle, already alluded to. The sisters feel no need to enlarge what can be done well, only if done small. Adding wings to wings, swelling the staff, more often than not wreaks havoc on the original intent— loving care of the ill. Whose law is that? In any case, Marianne Moore stated it years ago in somewhat different terms: "When excellence is the intent, to add is to subtract." Indeed.

The death managers are likewise absent. This is an inflexible rule in a bending universe. There are no state snoops because there is no state money. It is as simple as that. Freedom from the state is seen as freedom to do one's work. In a deeper sense, it is the freedom of the hospital to be itself, to be other than an instrument of the state, even such a rare instrument as a decent state social service— presuming such a rarity to exist.

All this stubborn grace hatches a *rara avis* indeed. St. Rose's is an institution that calls itself Christian, and deserves to be so called. This, it strikes me, is the best gift of the hospital, whether to the dying or to those who serve them. The Christian sense of things, symbols gently applied for healing, a quintessential skill in foreseeing need or pain—this results in good teamwork, a necessary balance between mourning the newly dead and going on for the living.

And in the city, what a relief!

America, I reflect wryly, is the place where anything can be corrupted. Even (no pun intended) death. Even before the fact.

In 1972, upon release from prison, I taught at Union Seminary for a year. With a start, I noted in the seminary elevators frequent reference to seminars on death and dying. This, while Nixon's savage carpet bombing of Vietnam, the bombing of the dikes, the spoliation of nature, were proceeding apace. And so far as I could learn, not an official or unofficial theological cry was being raised on, say, the death and dying of Vietnamese children.

We corrupt our sense of reality by sentimentalizing it.

Such excess erupts, for example, when we zero in on one aspect of things to the neglect of another; e.g., separating the facts of domestic death (occurring in the course of nature) from the facts of death abroad (inflicted, unrequited.) Thus, it was conceivable during the war that air force officers, in off hours, after successful bombing runs, or as part of their R and R, could attend seminar sessions sponsored by their chaplains on death and dying. The codicils of all this are truly horrific and, in my judgment, go to the heart of matters. That is to say, for war crime one is urged to read "official assignment"; for compassion, "applicable only to the blood line"; for the burning of children, "inevitable enemy casualty." And for theology, read—what?

The abstractions poison the soul, reduce our lives and deaths to market commodities, subject death itself to the technicians of death, whether psychological or technological. It is all, in fact, one: the brutalizing of ourselves, the degradation of language.

I am trying to suggest that we are inevitably sentimental until we become political, especially in matters of life and death. Our understanding, our caring, are summoned to embrace the fate of all, the common weal and woe. And when, at length, our sense of death has reached outward to embrace the enemy, the stranger, the outcast, dissolving petty differences and distance, and declared its peace with all creation—at that point we may claim a human sense that is something more than a threat or a bared weapon.

And in the instance of cancer, such a sense allows us to travel gracefully from fact to metaphor. Better still, to oscillate beween the two, touching each pole, the cancer close at hand, the dying across the world; the cancer at St. Rose's, the dying, the perennial dying of the survivors of Hiroshima.

Before the scourge of cancer, our civilization is largely helpless. We are, in fact, in the plight of the original sinner seeking to extirpate original sin. War upon war on cancer (the violent imagery is itself instructive) has been indeed declared and conducted—wars hot and cold. But the forays have resulted, for all their research and money, in ever more cancer.

Indeed, the cancer question widens, fact and mystery, as nuclear technology overshadows it. Thefts of plutonium, hideously inventive engines of mass killings, misuse of resources and talents, dangers of low radiation, a trapped and enfeebled war economy and, above all and permeating all, a spiritual stagnation that forbids us even tentative access to our own faith—these are a few penalties which the care and feeding of nuclear demons wring from us.

For the first time in history, the fate of humanity itself stands on a fail-safe basis, nicely calibrated, weapon for weapon, our side and theirs, a worldwide tension and terror. The question of "who can win" is wiped away by the paw of Mars; who now can survive?

The threat to existence is by no means idly issued. It is, but for an act of God, all but assured of execution, backed by the nicest proof imaginable—weapons apt to consummate the deed. So we live on—on borrowed time. Plain good luck, here and there a sane act of one or another leader drawing back from the verge (as in the Russian response to the Kennedy provocation), terrorism controlled, barely, by the greater terror of nation-states; for some thirty-five years these have given us an illusion of safety, cowering under the iron umbrella of "deterrence."

Deterrence did not deter; it eventually died, to be replaced by the apter gunslinging macho of "first strike." Today we are hostages to leaders who themselves are hostages—to past follies, to new weapons, to bunkers and stockpiles, to national frenzies, to stalking myths, dusted off and set in wilder motion, security, free world, Salt II. . .

I bring this up because something clumsily called the "politics of cancer" presses upon us. St. Rose's Home has become an apt image of our country and world. If a single nuclear device is detonated over any city of the planet (one out of tens of thousands of nukes which lie about the world), those who perish at the flash point may well be

accounted lucky. Those who survive will die also, gradu-
ally, after mutilation, bloodletting, thirst, nausea, of blood
cancer.

Cancer has thus become, as some forty mini-Pentagons
across the world testify, a hellish vocation of humanity.
Beyond the hospital, the metaphor. Before the catastrophe,
the warning. In the race toward oblivion, half the horror is
getting there. Day by day, in New York and elsewhere, the
poor drop by the wayside, emblems of things to come. The
poisoning of air and water and food strikes them down.
And in their fate we may read our own.

At present, some twelve orderlies at St. Rose's are
Catholic Workers. Several have been jailed in recent years
for resisting the nuclear arms race or nuclear energy plants.
They bring to the care of the cancer patients a sense of
impending showdown, a realism desperately required as an
ingredient of compassion, of sanity itself.

We live with the unknown, if we live at all.

A hideously deformed technology demands something
else, that we live with a curious version of "the known," the
threat, the myth, the inexorable, the (as they love to say)
facts of life today. In sum, we are to accept a bleak military,
political, economic fate, a botched mockup of reality. We
are condemned to it; we are to live in it, the "real world," as
in a cage.

In the cage, moreover, is a child's rocking horse; on it we
swing away, off balance, distracted, feverish, doomed. Like
the child in D. H. Lawrence's story, we rock until we die.

At St. Rose's, an entirely different story. Those who
work there, those who suffer and die there, must live with
the unknown, in trust. The Dream stops here. There are no
gods skulking in corners, no cures. There may indeed be a
true God; but in this place He refuses to act, is silent.

Patients who arrive on their feet, some with a quixotic last-ditch will to "get well," quickly or slowly collapse, fade out. Others arrive in extremis; they fall like moths before a frost. But whatever their condition, or the resignation or anger or bewilderment that marks their families, one takes a stand at their side, a stand in favor of life, infinitely precious and fragile. And waits. And hopes.

A restoration of balance goes on. I think of it as weights placed nicely on a scale, a Catholic correction of the literally unbalanced world. The more life is rendered cheap, held in low esteem, made expendable, made subject to blasphemous property and bullish dollar, nullified in the womb, disposed of through gas and electric voltage, shoved over the abyss of war, the more victims demanded by rancor and revenge—the more crucial it seems to me that we intervene. We must declare our trust in life at that exact point where life is most assailed, put to naught. Thus, in accord with a law of nature itself, a law of balance and compensation, Christians belong in resistance—at the Pentagon, on the Bowery, at abortion mills, and in the prisons. And in cancer wards.

I think of the cliffs of Block Island, assaulted and attrited by the sea's fury. Each winter, several feet of the promontory fall into the tides. Every attempt to stop the land loss fails; tons of brush are dumped over the cliffs, grasses sown, sea walls thought of. But nothing avails, so far. Nature rips away. Home owners, the lucky ones, move their houses inland, gain a few years.

But if you are attentive, raise your eyes, a marvel meets you, a strange compensation. The far side of the island slopes gently to the sea, in wondrous beaches. And, there, the land builds and builds. The old lighthouse that once stood at the sea's verge is now some half-mile inland; what was once sea is a wilderness of dunes and grasses.

I think, under this image of trust, compensation. The dying, worn down, caving in, their bodies puffed or emaciated, the odor of sweat and nauseous decay—all is but one side of things, the "things which are seen."

You make a covenant with the unseen side of things as you watch death's invasion. It is all immensely strange, awesome, real. The covenant, the trust, is placed in life and the life giver; in a promise. But the trust is also in the nature of things, without evidence; it is offered only in hints and starts. You cannot make the covenant directly with the invisible, the presence that presses and covertly hides. You must swear the oath of trust with those who seem least able to fulfill it, least able to act as proxy for its Principal. Which is to say, you make it with the dying. You hold a hand, look into failing eyes, muster what words you can, or better, perhaps, say nothing.

Out of the depths. No other way. There may have been a time, almost certainly there was, when caring for cancer patients was a fairly exotic work. It was possible to place one's self at a reasonably safe distance from such a fate. There were protagonists and there were victims, the ill and the healthy; the lines were clean.

There was as yet no culture of cancer, so to speak, a spore on the winds. There was no plutonium, there had been no Hiroshima. There was not even a Pentagon; wars were ironically "conventional."

Metaphorically, as well, we were not yet "nuked." Families were not splitting, things were holding, making sense. Or so it was believed. The poor of New York who were stricken with cancer could be successfully isolated. They were transported by boat to Welfare Island in the East River, there to die out of sight, out of mind. Clearly, the city was coping with its domestic lepers. Or so it was believed.

All that is changed. The cancer situation now is one of stark and simple mutuality; those hands we swear by all but draw us with the urgency of truth or death into their darkness.

A bitter truth. We, our children, our fair land, the sea-drenched cliffs and beaches—all are endangered. The days pass, the danger nears; it is clear by now that only an act of God can snatch us from the folly of death, universal, self-inflicted.

An act of God. The expression stops me short. It normally serves to preclude responsibility, not to invoke it. God's act is thought of as a kind of court of last resort, a hair's-breadth snatch at the end of things. But all this is unbiblical, demeaning to God and ourselves. The act of God is simply a covenant in which, hand in hand, we bespeak our trust in God, our stake in the world and its creatures, in truthful living and good outcome. Come what may. The act of God is enacted by us, here and now, each day; or it is not.

For my part, I believe the vainglorious and violent will not inherit the earth, to its utmost destruction. In pursuance of that faith, my friends and I take the hands of the dying in our hand. And some of us travel to the Pentagon, and others live on the Bowery and serve there, and others speak unpopularly and plainly of the fate of the unborn and of convicted criminals. It is all one.

Thus, acts of trust render us trustworthy. Let the covenant be verified elsewhere. The act is, after all, primarily an act of God. For ourselves, our trust is not merely that the dying voyage into another orbit of existence, but that they "live, in Christ Jesus."

Nor does that other world, that "great ring of pure and endless light," stand at great distance from us. It is other, but it also interposes, illumines, presses, warms, signals. Its heart, its God, is also our God. And the life He vindicates, rewards, restores, elsewhere, beyond our ken, He would also have vindicated, restored, defended, here and now. The act of God is also the act of humans, ourselves.

Paul Goodman wrote somewhere that his respect for Christians was based on their utterly crazy comprehension of the last day. Perhaps he was right, I am not sure. I think that what we have to offer today is an utterly crazy comprehension of this day, of the day-to-day, of the simultaneous acceptance and taming of the apocalyptic fury. I am not sure the day-to-day is not the last day.

We are indeed, as a hundred rumblings underfoot remind us, stepping gingerly in the mine field of the end of things. This is no news to anyone who walks in prophetic bones; hardly news, certainly not good news. Can we make of a sorry time good news? "I am with you." We must deterrorize the terror, by an act of God, our act.

Let us tell our heart; we will swear our covenant anew. We will hold the hand of the dying. It is an act of sublime trust, of land trust, of water trust, of trust in God, of trust in one another.

The covenant reverberates in the womb; the endangered unborn, surely the "least of these," hear our voice. Please trust us, little ones, we hold your hand.

The covenant reaches into prisons and death rows. Trust us; we do not believe that murder casts out murder.

The covenant says to all: Stand in our circle. We declare that humanity itself is a nuclear-free zone.

God does not walk away from such an oath. Neither would we.

Chapter 1

HOW IT ALL GOT STARTED

Sister said, on my first arrival, "We take patients only when the doctors give up. At that point, all we can offer is a place to die, to be cared for, an atmosphere really."

We visited the chapel.

She gave me a cup of coffee.

One of the orderlies came out from behind the bed curtains as we were going through a ward. He was doing bed care for an emaciated old man, breathing like a whistle through a hollow shinbone. Sister went on: "We have trouble finding the right people to work here, you can't look on it like a nine-to-five job. People don't die on schedule any more than they get born on schedule."

(Everywhere I go I have a sense of being "shown through"—except when I go to jail. One gets a feeling after a while one is being shown through the universe. Isn't this an awful metaphor, being a tourist of existence, a freeloader? Maybe when I get some dirt on my hands the feeling will vanish.)

Sister: "There's a big vogue in 'dying' now. We don't have a psychiatrist on staff; don't think we need one."

Fifty patients. A laboratory in dying, a corner (literally) out of the world. In the world, birth and death get denatured, befogged, reified, secularized, surveyed, televised, interviewed—out of their skull, out of all recognition, self-knowledge, access to wisdom.

> Creator spirit come, that I may come true.
> My tears, my tears fall in the night.

Went back, Ascension Thursday. A minor mauling on subway and bus. I kept wondering, in a lightheaded way, what might lie ahead. Sister met me. In honor of Jesus Going Up, we ascended in the elevator.

The head nursing sister met me. One thing I admire here, they take you at your word. Which is to say, beds and lockers ready for scrubbing with disinfectant, mattresses to be moved off and on again in the men's ward. We collected the cleaning aids; I went at it. It isn't hard work by any standards I know; some of the beds have an electric lifting apparatus and an orderly helped me get things hoisted off and on.

In gritty old New York, the place is irreproachably clean. I kept an eye out for the faces and voices of patients, met one and another intermittently as I swabbed away. Sister is easy on the pace, but she wants perfection at the end of each phase. I slowly got it; beds should be exactly made up, mitered corners sharp as a razor cut. . .

Lunch in the workers' dining room at twelve. There I met the silent and carefree, the jokers and volunteers and steadies. Good meal, of which I had stomach only for a bowl of soup.

All the patients who speak have stories to tell—endlessly. No wonder, most of them have lived long lives and hunger for a chance to tell it all. Printer, maintenance man, sea captain, cook—they've come to the end of every job and skill, the end of the laborious furrow. Into a small cove in a racing channel, the New York run. Now they have time, time hanging heavy on their hands, a dead weight among the turbulent living. The city is studded with hospitals, high and mighty as the Trade Towers, consecrated in the main, to help us die as we live—too fast, not too thoughtful; die faster, we need the pillows!

Here is a difference, I'd judge from first experience. The sisters set another rhythm going. Slow down New Yorkers, you'll go even slower soon; why not learn the skill, grab time by the forelock? Why be dumped into eternity like someone pushed from a fast train onto a siding, tumbling along like a poor weed in the wind?

David is going, almost gone. Thirty-three years old. Eyes milky, jaw open, he's horrifically persuasive, miming the dead. Sister works over him like a newborn. "He panics if he doesn't know what's coming. But when I make a move and tell him, he's an angel."

So he is, hands clenched on his chest like a crab's claws, head thrown back as though snatching at a waterfall. And his poor shaved head sprouting big knots and warts like a rotten log. There'd better be another world, he doesn't have much going for him in this one.

And Jason the sea captain across the hall. He has a single, knobby point to his head, off to the side, like a foolish Martian cap gone awry. Dying of brain tumor; his wife is taking a breather in the country; for two years she commuted while hope lasted, from Jersey to New York. . . . He held my hand, his thumb stroked my palm, his poor, wide eyes slowly focusing on my face after a great trouble and blinking, like a dog looking for a friend in a subway blur.

How I grow to love them all! I had a few sinking moments this week, wondering if a day in the death house might be too much to bear. It was an old familiar feeling; I connected it almost immediately to a day early on in Danbury jail, when the thought of months of lockup ahead all but stopped my heart. And then you went on, because go on you must. Something like it here, except (a huge exception, indeed) here the doors open from the outside. But I can only report, impersonally as the weather, the place, the people, fit me like a glove. Prosit.

The families come and go, restive, subdued; now and again, a little kid breaks loose from the pack, makes a run for it, finds some acquiescent soul to bounce off. In the adult faces, a guilty look of those still on their feet, those who must look for help after a mighty try at home care, long months of lifting, cleaning, night watch, above all hoping; for the "best" that never arrives. And the thought all but written in their eyes: "Have I done all I could. . . ?"

So a kind of hybrid existence begins. Sister introduces me around: Father Dan. They take a quick gander; there's that sidelong pursed look of the Irish: "Come on now you're kidding me!" My old clothes no recommendation; no black, no collar, unprepossessing frame, the face that fails to launch a single lifeboat. The Catholics shake hands; reluctant or right on, you sense the weak wonderment: "Well, well, anything's possible these days, isn't it?"

Old Herman's eighty-four, a face like a stuck mule. He can dream up more jobs around and about this person than you could shake a baton at. One morning he gave me a forty-minute tour of his dream life, mostly nightmares about being locked in cages underground. Though he hurried on to assure me the dreams stopped once he got to the hospital. Oh yes indeed, no more of that! . . . Then he was yelling for help once more; this time it was to change his shit bag or his piss bag or some other suspended aid.

As they approach death you easily imagine their faces dead. This doesn't, in fact, require much imagination at all—a plain futurable.

I want to make of these days what the old liturgy calls "a perpetual remembrance." The phrase is not about merit or winning favor, but about letting go.

I would like to let go, with each of these lives, something of myself, something of that spar, clung to desperately, futilely, against nature and right order. Something of ego, excess, too much. To refuse rescue, go down willingly, even joyfully, when the current rises. And to test the current before diving in, to sense without knowing that the other dark shore is also a world of the living.

Walking that thin line. One orderly called in sick this morning, too shaken, I think. The job's getting to him, the exhaustion of living among the dying. Let it pass, let it all go. My back is like a piece of firewood hit by a dull ax. To allow the world in, just short of hellishly too much. . .

I'm beginning to sense it; you have to be in good form spiritually to work here. The routine is harsh, frayed tempers, abuse from the ill. There's no eternal light flickering around these beds. The scene is strictly of this world, with those few small exceptions here and there: the tenderness of a dying hand, a spurt of passion connecting. In spite of yourself, your heart leaps. Can it be that even I could be a landmark for someone casting off?

The patients come in, more or less in the throes, nearly all pretending ignorance of impending fate. Sister said quite decidedly, "Most know the facts." Some of them hide it from themselves, others cling to this or that ambiguous statement or downright lie of a doctor.

You could see the duplicity in the eager face of old John, leaning out of his chair to ask, "What did the doc say about my left foot?"

Theater of the absurd. His gut is a pot of rotten tripe,

and he's asking, "What did the doc say about my etc.?"
Sister plays the game, an old hand. "He said fine, fine; it
oughtn't to be giving you much pain." He falls back
satisfied; someone's willing to play along with him: "Right,
sister, no pain at all, at all."

You can't cry all the time, you have to laugh
sometimes—even from the wheelchair you're trundling to-
ward the last day. You push it out into the parking lot, so to
speak, and load the groceries and meat (especially the meat,
so to speak) into the back seat, and Tiger Lady drives off
humming the tiger rag. For your courtesies as checkout
boy, she waves that manicured left hand with the death-
white, inch-long nails, she smiles that man-eating smile.
You roll the empty cart back to the meat counter, more
thoughtful than usual. That smile! Her Impala loaded up
with dead meat for the freezer, for the fryer. And she sized
you up, too; her smile was a tenderizer, she likes her meat
aged on the hoof. You'll keep.

I'm inclined to stay mum as yet about working in the
hospital. One day a week is a minicontribution at best, less
said the better. And in any case, one's insight has to go
further than this or that death by cancer. Namely, I hope
the whole show is not terminal. Certainly, the Pentagon is
working like mad toward "termination": you, I, the chil-
dren, the unborn, everybody, every living thing. No won-
der there's a shadow at the back of my skull whispering:
Watch out, things can only get worse.

It's a darkness that admits only the faintest crack of
light—salvation. And in its wake, the nightmare urges
modesty.

The day of the Lord's Ascension. A reminder of the
other side (something other than death; the liturgy says on

this day He "took captivity captive"; the death that put death out of business). We know virtually nothing about that mystery, that glory; no maps are extant of that other side: except we have His word, His absence, His world, to assure us another side exists. And one must add: Of certain aspects of this side we surely know too bloody much!

Here I go taking another dose of "this side." It's also a cry—His side had better exist! I look on it as a wager of sorts. I'd like to pick up the bet; for the sake of those who careen, faster and more dreadfully, to the brink of the world.

All bets on! It doesn't make the outcome any clearer; it gives some ballast and sense to the trip.

In proportion as death is your enterprise, you're bound to be less interesting to the living; in the root sense of "interesting," i.e., that which is of deep concern to many. We want life. We want it even for those who work against it, who kill, who believe in killing as an act of social usefulness, personal enhancement, political savvy; those also who do the works of death (safely at a distance from the results): that phalanx of researchers, scientists, engineers, for whom bomb-making is a "living." I long to enlarge the scope of life until it includes everyone from soldiers to priests, a spectrum by no means arbitrary or easily entered. . .

We resist the death game (by way of radical understanding, resistance) in proportion as we connect with the life game (by way of embrace, ecstasy).

I note, too, a cultural heist; big deals and spurious values result only in inhuman, bloodletting conduct. A like heist would persuade us that death is of small moment indeed; in the sense, at least, that the death of many "invisible" people is regrettable, but required—in the nature of things. Such are considered subjects of legitimate social experiment, to be used and cast aside in the course of the long march toward nirvana. But how many will survive till arrival, even supposing the plan is anything more than a vile mirage? Let us seek purity in each step, each stage; let the outcome take care of itself.

As I lose the gift of tears, I also gain a kind of surreal clarity of understanding. Like a sleepwalker in a high noon without shadows, by Chirico. This is a loss of balance, a loss beyond words. I want to weep, and I want to stop talking. But they invite me to all sorts of places, to talk, talk. And no one, of course, wants a holy weeper around. The last big groaner I met in my life was Paul Goodman. Maybe I have little to weep for; but he had lost his son.

I note about professional talkers something I notice about professional anyones: Death, including the death of Jesus, is a matter of relative abstraction. No great loss, no great tragedy, a wordly indifference. And then, by way of contrast, my dying Irishman at the hospital, who tells me through his paper-thin, paper-white lips, "I don't know how Jesus could have borne with being crucified."

Scratch an American, California to New York, and find someone who wants to weep, needs to. Or at least to undergo the foreplay of tears; to unload, to talk and talk. Life backs up, rises on itself, too much to bear. No one to talk to, everything to weep for. Not idly did we once learn about the gift of tears. It is still granted when one is dropped into a lachrymal desert. Springs break out, what a breakthrough!

We had a party following a mass. I felt so at home; occasion and place were gentle, accepting, right. And I was led to think of other liturgies, other places—charades in outer space. Surely there ought to be something more life-giving to celebrate than mere professionalism, or worse, mutual institutionalism. It's like lighting the gas flame in the basket of a hot-air balloon; you go up briefly, and down inevitably.

A Franciscan brother has joined us, an R.N. He seems devoted and capable; drove me uptown at the end of the day. He's trying to study theology and get ordained; we talked about the idiocies of certain incanted words today, *obedience* among them. He's been kicked raw by the Big Ones, hangs on with bitten fingers.

The Irish end sad, so sad. The men die, the women live alone and nurse their fires in rotting neighborhoods. Through the long months of final "settlement," they travel long distances and then sit with their men and read the *Irish Echo* over a thermos of tea. The faces say, like a speechless chorus, "Bad, getting worse!"

Many of those abed have the same witless refrain: "Help of God I'll be getting home soon. . . ." They know they'll never leave here alive, but the Irish are big on fantasy, hopes that go nowhere. Do they believe what they want you so desperately to believe? Do they know that you know something different?

All the death! It seems to go right over my head. I have at times to remind myself that others are tasting death, a bitter reality, that there is great sorrow in the air. Yet I have no tears, not a one. I keep asking myself if this is hardness of heart. Or can it be that I've passed beyond death's terror? I think, something of both.

I marvel at the orderlies. The best of them scold and hug and laugh at the dying and cut their hair and nails and wash them toe to crown, all with marvelous style and panache. Others are earnest and slow and good as gold and can't imagine the tip of their own noses. Such an atmosphere of love! I write this hesitantly, an old hand practiced in the death of practically everything.

The hospital is surrounded with a tough barricade of public housing paved with broken glass, kids in the streets, music blaring, life pushing close. Drug addicts abound, but not one foray has ever been made into the hospital. The housing folk are superstitious, I'm told; call the place the "death house," and take the long way around.

I was sitting by the window, a book by Kierkegaard in hand. Came up this old number, self-propelled. He's a great one for reading, finds himself a corner somewhere, always with a book. He has the face of a hermit-pope, calm, waiting to pass the frontier, credentials in hand. What was I reading?

I said, "A famous theologian."

"What does he have to say?"

"He says the church ought not play footsie with the state, but hew to its own path and conviction."

He listened in silence, craning past my shoulder in silence, the traffic of the highway, the East River beyond.

"Well, who doesn't know that?"

"Very few seem to know it, he says, judging from the way things go. He marvels at how few Christians there are."

"Who doesn't know that?"

Later on, crouching in bed like a pope in his hermitage, he said, "It's just like the mafia. Play with that, you can't be a Christian. But such ideas are unpopular; I agree with your theologian what's-his-name."

Came out of the subway at Chambers Street into bright May sunlight. The whole city seemed to have paused in mid-beat, everyone ga-ga over the young climber inching up the Trade Tower. I made my way east; everything was stopped dead, the human fly was inching upward on the immense vertical grid. Those that couldn't see, had radios pasted to their ears.

Then I went on and into the hospital, where life so to speak is strictly horizontal, no more climbing up anything—except maybe Jacob's ladder. And the dying were listening, too, the TV's and radios hopping with the unfinished climb.

Mac died unexpectedly this morning; a stroke took him off cleanly, just as the sun slipped the horizon. He told me a week ago at some length that he had been a school super in four or five big city plants; he seemed vigorous and in command.

I began washing and changing beds. The effect of Mac's death was heavy in the air, orderlies noticeably quieter, patients quiet. I cleaned out the old sea captain's locker; he hove in to claim his stuff, the locker packed with junk. He kept mumbling to himself, "Bow wow," all bark, no bite; he'd never be able to find anything in place again. We let him put the stuff back to suit himself. That was that. He huffed awhile, then quieted down.

I've seen it today, remarked it before. The face of the dying is almost pure convex. The eyes like dead sockets, the mouth shaped to silence. Every one of them, my father and mother and that poor dying man today, looks alike. We are drawn from the womb into the muddle of earth; we carry one face. The dying look more alike than the newborn, who bring into the world some identity tag; carrot hair or pug nose. But the dead are one saffron, one used parchment, a Dead Sea scroll ready for its sealed jar.

A long talk with the man who distrusted theologians. I offered him a cup of coffee; he was in his wheelchair in the small parlor; he warmed up to the idea, and we sat there for some time. He wanted to sketch the gulls disporting over the East River in the rain that drowned the day. Said, "The *National Geographic* ought to show something of their form." So he paged through, seeking his ideal gull. I told him of the Wisconsin lake I had seen last October, the quarter-million Canadian geese that claimed the lake country en route to Louisiana. Their magnificent strength, endurance, wing spread, fascinated him.

(He's the one whose skull and ears and stance bring back my father so uncannily; that and his skinny, forward look as he wheels about, always on his own, among the survivors.)

Told me his father was an artist who worked in many New York churches, in the old immigrant Romantic style. "They're all covered over now, no one wants the saints around. Churches are more like synagogues." Prosit. Was his father native-born? "He was born in Poland. An army man, cashiered for some delict or other, landed here." Had he gone to art school? "I think for six months or so. But he simply had the talent, that was all." He spread his bony hands, it was like a man illustrating flight.

Bob talked a bit today. I noticed the terrible red potato on his skull has changed shape again. Now it looks almost ready to split in two livid parts. It literally fumes, a break-out force of its own. . . . He spoke of his sea voyages slowly, in measure, with much difficulty. "I carried a cargo of tapioca and rice from Molucca, left off food, rope, cloth; I sailed passengers, too." He speaks when and to whom he wants.

He will die at thirty-four, when the buoy strikes; and with a patience and slow, moving dignity that befit a sea captain. In spite of the horrid mushroom flowering on his brow. We held hands, neither of us ashamed. I wish I could weep.

Arrived soaked in the rain, left at four, a second soaking. Bus and subway; people battling like the damned to go north, to go south. It rains and rains tonight as though Earth were a waterwheel under a cosmic Niagara.

Rose got to the hospital somehow from Brooklyn. Her Bernie put aside the *News* for a moment to greet her. Al, who speaks no English, glommed on to the paper. There ensued a Marat Sade battle. Bernie speaks only strangled vowels; something of his fury came though: "Daking brivet proberdy!" Al, gesticulating in repentance, wheeled around to surrender the sheet. . . . Bernie's daughter brought their dog in. A vague sense of incongruity, clarified later; how many dogs are allowed in hospitals? This one, spiked like a porcupine, noses about in the manner of small growlers. No one seems to give him a second thought. He keeps trying to jump on Bernie's bed. "Just like the old days," Rose said.

They fastened a pair of gauze-and-wood paddles over the hands of old Jimbo, who was getting rambunctious, trying to climb out of bed alone, tearing his clothes off. Now he looks comic, like a big, helpless platypus; but with a sweet smile, a shade of barking devilry. After all, I reflect, who wouldn't have dotty spells now and then, so shortly before the send-off? Indeed, the end is written on the walls, large; and every meal, every passage of the drug cart, change of diapers, each is a reminder of the real work to be done; dying, a work of art, unrepeatable.

The old guy in the middle ward lies there with marmoreal dignity. He's all but blind, over ninety years old, has a smile to wring the heart. He was a cook for over sixty years at the same Wall Street restaurant. "We served only one meal per day; they came in and went out fast; eating was an interruption from chasing the buck."

If I stop at his bed for a moment, he senses I'm there. He stares past me and thanks me with great civility "for visiting me." Reward enough, that smile.

A new man, broken hip half-mended, life half-jostled out of him after an ambulance ride from the Bronx. "I've had my fill of these hospitals," he pants. He's been captive in five of them. When he raised his arm to shake hands, I saw a big tattoo on his forearm, three initials and a tombstone! "That's for my wife," is all he said.

Why do they show so little meanness or fretfulness? Is all the ginger eaten out of them by drugs, cut out with the knife? You see good smiles, a large measure of peaceableness. There's a sense of waiting in the air. And since almost every ward has one death each week, the waiting is laden, heavy. The dark angel passes, the sword unsheathed.

To see Mike trimming the fingernails of a dying man! An invisible gesture, the gracful bow which life sweepingly makes—not in subservience to death, but to life. The mortician spruces up the dead—"the dead burying the dead" is the way the gospel puts it. But this is indeed something else. . . . The body is paradisaical; it goes on its journey in beauty and finesse—*ad unguem!* The old man winces, twitches his hand away; the cuticle is grown over and inflamed. Mike pushes it gently back in a half-moon sweep. A small matter, a service beyond call; and for that reason, beyond praise. We may go in rags; indeed we all go in rags;

but let us go cleanly, summon our dignity and straighten our spines.

Seven died in seven days. How cold this sounds on paper, yet with what a pang I recall those faces, most of them old, scarred, ravaged, tired, beyond the hope and skills of this world, images of the plight of all.

I brought a book to Henry. His face lit up like a soulful skull. Later he said, "Why did you think to bring it to me?" Said, "Because I noticed you're a great reader, and I thought you'd enjoy it." And he, "You're right; if I could quash the TV around here, and get my bag changed at six in the morning, life would be perfect. . . ."

A retired cop came in yesterday, died last night. And the old, set-faced, spastic man died, a mercy. So did Tattoo Joe. The sea captain lingers on. They keep his brain tumor swathed in bandages; it looks like a grotesque tea caddy atop his head, or one of those minihats you fasten with a rubber band under your chin, to go to a silly party.

Everyone cringes at putting restraints, however gentle, on patients. There's a sense that such things are a sorry last resort. The Great Restrainer shortly arrives for the main act; and who wants to initiate a rehearsal?

One old guy, I'm convinced, shits for pure spite in the virginal sheets of his bed; then tears off his pajamas and wallows about like a pig in an estuary. This is all the more remarkable since, ten minutes before, he was entertaining visitors and playing model patient. The fun was on, the shit didn't hit. Then, whammy! Anyway, the orderly took a lot of abuse and played things cool. But he had to end up tying on a pair of those ping-pong paddles which, in the land of primates, would pass for hands; but which, here, are simply grotesque and humiliating. The old boy sets about with all might and main to free himself. But to no avail.

A spirit of "hands off" prevails when someone decides to go for broke. It could hardly be called resignation, too fierce for that. It's a longing to hasten what impends, to dare death to come on fast and clean. Meantime, keep your distance. . . . Old Mike warned me off when I came up timorously inquiring if he wanted anything. It was as though he were swinging a censor of hot coals and incense as they do in the Greek mass to create a sacred circle; the message: Keep off! Keep back! He's like a building afire. He wants to go up in a conflagration, no debris.

Everything goes in cycles; was it Pythagoras said so? And Jesus paid tribute to seasons and all manner of turnabout, day and night, harvest and planting. . . . We are at present in a cycle of crazies. It can be announced calmly, though I feel as though I've been sucked into a moon crater. As beyond doubt, at times, I am. Meantime, as the poet says, I hope to cope.

It is not so much the cheap, multiplied death strikes me, whether in hospital or street. (The news today is that Son of Sam has been seized.) Captive, captivation, both part of our history. I think tonight, with all the weird rejoicing and relief in the city, mixed as it is with despair and revenge, something archetypal, subterranean, is abroad—a horror that walks by day and stalks by night.

Just to be foolish among the foolhardy, I thought; what if a president or general or cabinet member had been seized *in flagrante?* A public authority, let us say, who went beyond the "call of duty," beyond the law, ordered villagers in

Vietnam shot or napalmed, ordered bombings of hospitals, etc., during our terrible discarded decade. . .

Weep, weep my soul, the mass murderers attend church, attend to their children; the poor suburban and urban crazies are taken by stealth, subjected to psychiatric punctures. And the mad society heaves a breath of relief; the experts prowl about, separating sane sheep from mad goats. From such sanity O Lord deliver us!

An old black man lies low like a hand-carved, ebony image. He'll go any time now. Meantime, his family visits him every Thursday at least. I praise him here, which is a little like praising God, redundant; and at the same time, one of the chief joys of life.

Soon, our man will have dispensed with all crude proximities and voids; and God will proceed to praise him. And that's when life begins.

Another late arrival, an Irishman with the face of a newly dug spud; all bumps and hollows, indiscriminate. He matches wits with the Hispanic orderly; it's all ice and fire, in good spirits.

One could say, in truth, most of the dying put on a good face; which, in these cases, I am convinced, is something more than show or ploy. People die well, unless prevented. Could this be extrapolated to read, "People live well, unless prevented?" On the nature of prevention, as on the meaning of *unless* (moral suasion or violent jolt), few are agreed.

A deaf mute, aged forty-two. Literally, from top to foot, no wholeness in him. His hair was matted and unkempt, his feet like horned hooves. (This is a fairly common occurrence; people arrive in such condition—from families who can no longer cope, from dreadful nursing homes and hospitals.) Anyway, two orderlies set to work to repair the neglect. I held the poor man firm, side left then right, while someone cut his hair. Then another carefully tended to his feet.

One gets into a routine in the business of serving, cleaning, stripping beds, getting ready for the next arrival. With me it's a fusion of bewilderment and physical training—something like what I went through in prison years ago. One functions badly, but with all one's will screwed up to the sticking point. Thinks ruefully: I may not bring this off with grace; but, what the hell, in such circumstances gracelessness is next to godliness.

I wonder: Wouldn't things be easier if they died like the mad folk of *King of Hearts* or *Marat Sade?* But they die exactly like the mimes of '77 or '78 or '79, i.e., flashing back at our eyes with hand mirrors, the cold lumen of the minisoul we hardly knew we had.

Practically no one screams or curses.

The Irish fascinate me, for obvious reasons. Moody and stubborn, jaws and backsides firm against the Windy Prevailer. The Jews are scared or unconvinced, they walk away and get blunderbussed somewhere down the pike. The Spanish are dangerous, gamesmen; they want some fun; they write a script close to the Greek tragic scheme: strict beginning, middle, and end.

But all this is only a middling reflex on what is essentially unencumbered, uncontained, like a Johnstown flood. The sisters keep the watch, night and day; the flood doesn't sweep people off, so to speak, it traps them imperceptibly while they sleep; they drown, they awaken dead. Is this because the sisters take the first cruel brunt, the first wave, to themselves?

The deaf mute Thomas died after ten days. Sister told how, in his last hours, when he slept most of the time, she would come by and notice him sign-talking in his dreams. He was telling his dreams into empty air as he died. I never before heard of such an episode among the dying; neither had anyone I talked to.

(When I told this in a group some time later, one alligator asked with wide jaws, as though the story were a steaming morsel, "Well, what did he SAY?").

The sweet old man who lay there so patiently—the cancer a purple patch all over him, like a badly gotten up clown—is gone. Turn him over, he groaned like Hamlet's father in purgatorial fires. But he would thank you with pitiful vehemence, press his gratitude; it was his last will, we were all major beneficiaries.

One of the few who brought up the subject of dying was a bony-faced Irishman. He said something noncommittal like, "Cancer all over me, what can I do? . . ." He had a restaurant in Jamaica, same location thirty-five years, "Now look at me!" I said something lame like, "You're going first, we're all to come after. . ."

I've found here not a lot of stark talk about dying, but the hundreds of ways in which people signal or sign to you; "I'm on a long journey, won't you come along, as nearly, as best you can, as far as allowed? . . ."

My dear eighty-five-year-old is sinking; he throws his long, skinny legs over the bars of the bed and keeps calling for Catherine. He's about to launch his boat, spring is here! So it is, so it is, in dark waters to be sure; and as to Catherine, she is long gone, vanished over those waters, without a trace.

The wife of an old Irisher greets me with that deep-grained malice and sweet talk one comes to be wary of—thin honey, lots of vinegar. She loves "faatheh." So she says, but I have reason to doubt it. Love this down-and-out "preesht" who scrubs wheelchairs and careens about with mugs of coffee in hand? . . . Her old man is past all this flimflam; he bellows away like Con Ed's horn across the river, his troubles other than me. She's long and quick on his virtues. How he ushered at Saint Mary's thirty-eight years, more than that, always visiting the poor. . . . He was a stationary engineer all his life; you should see the hundreds of tons of coal he shoveled. . . . There's nothing like a near end to bring on a rush of perceived virtue, like sandblasting a blackened monument.

You come home almost too tired to think, a great sadness laid on your heart. And you think: At least I have a taste of the fate of millions who struggle for a toehold in the city, fight their way to work and back across the underground, all but ground under; that New York look of bare endurance, another day gone, here comes another blockbuster. . . . Robert Lowell's death in a cab, what a lonely passing for the half-mad poet who walked in and out of Catholicism like a ghost, looking for rest in waterless places—who, like so many, found little rest in the church or out of it. Life's fitful fever.

A party at the hospital. "Wasn't that somethin!" as mother used to aver. We were all maneuvered, chairs sideways, beds rolled somehow into a rather cramped room, the largest available, there to be served chicken and salads and trimmings. Eating with folk who, on the next round, will be downing angel food or manna; How soon, how soon? Meantime, some could eat, some could intravene, some could only sip their liquid, waiting glassy-eyed for the Knuckle at the door.

I loved it all, wondered, wanted to be part of it, eat, drink, and listen for the Knock. It's what we all do in any case, much of the time, though we have other names for the waiting game. And, compared with the storm that may be gathering, the rap-tap of that hand on the wood may be the sweetest, gentlest sound yet to break on mortal ears.

I'm fairly used by now to the sight of weak frames and greying faces. At least to the point where I can slide into their narrow line of vision without wreaking havoc—on them or myself. Little Ron continues to fail, as does almost everyone; but he keeps a good face on things. The old Creole goes badly; not merely that he can't hold his head up, but he rounds on others with so sour a spirit. . . . Do we go under in a better frame than the way we stayed afloat? I doubt it.

Old Fran greets me with a measured patrician air; he's parceling out his gestures like an ancient patrimony.

I dream a tribe stalked into the ward at midnight, on moccasins or
    bare soles.
They're dressed in dashikis and deerskins and long, sibilant,
    bizarre robes.
Skilled in the interpreting of dreams, they can draw a soul out of a
    body like ill humors.
See how one lights a flame in a crystal jar, another applies his
    mouth, bending to the open mouth of the dying one.
Another in the background catches a dream as it issues, smoke
    and light, from the eyes of the near dead. The dream has dark
    wings, an eagle look. It fed like a beak on unresisting flesh.
    They are taming the dream.
Yet another whispers commandingly to a barely breathing ser-
    pent that winds sinuously out of a nostril: "Go in, enter again."

Commands: Live. Imagine life. Imagine healing. Imagine the
death of your death, the resurrection of your life. . .
Another smears a sleeping face with a star of warpaint. "Arise,
arise," is all he whispers. Now the soul may join the constella-
tions leaping upward, a vast distance from his leaden-footed
illness. He has not walked a step in years. How he will super-
cede, surpass, fly.
The Year of the Cancer. All clocks stopped. The twentieth-
century roadrunners stopped too, impaled on the spiked hands
of time. They are drawn off now like dismembered meat over
the fires of death. Death has gone far—far enough.

The old salesman is all revved up. Body stopped cold,
tongue's in high gear.

His wife comes in, spiffy and mordant, hair blue as Betsy
Ross's banner. She sizes us up. By right she sits down. By
sufferance I sit down. He lies low. He signals me, pulls me
down to him, mouth to ear. "You know what, it's shit to be
in this place." I guffaw; he's so right it hurts, it helps. Wife
is not amused, she's missed something, leans forward.
"What did my husband say?" As though he's not there at
all, or I'm summoning his ghost on a ouija board.

I look at her. I wasn't there to edit the penultimate words
of anyone. "He said," I said, level as a pond, "he said it's
shit to be in this place."

Her true-blue, proper, suburban skull all but cracked.
"Oh, Father!" she wailed. Would she topple over back-
wards like a pile of melons? I feared mightily. But no, chic
uber alles. She suffered. She endured. She hoped I'd under-
stand, with a glance at the heavens that bespoke heroic
volumes, untold sufferance.

Now, it must be recalled, he was lying there in the ward,
connected to a strange umbilical, a plastic bag full of
above-mentioned detritus. Much time to memorize the clas-
sic text: "Remember folks, that detritus thou art, unto de-

tritus shalt return." While wife, though a loyal visitor to the morgue, was free to come and free to go, free to click her tongue at indiscretions, free to tend house and flowerbeds, to wait, perchance to dream. . .

Five weeks away in the summer, on the road. Then back, with a sinking heart, to count the vanished ghosts. . . And who should have shuffled off but old Fred, main character in the longest dying in anyone's memory here—seven years.

He lay there like a graven, forbidding image: transparent, waxen, a mold for the final bronze. He wore his own death mask for years and years. Ever since his thieving friend Oscar gave up the ghost, Fred gave up, too. He would utter not a syllable, nothing when I came in, nothing when I left. The same big hiatus always greeted me, an automatic yawn at the approach of the Big Sleep.

There lay Fred, there he lies no more. Seven years dying; that should indeed hurry him through the seven stories of the mythic mountain!

Then there was Mr. Williams, who used to shuffle about, carrying a plastic spittoon to the side of his face. He drizzled like a rain forest. It made you swallow dry; just to be near him took an enormous effort of will. But after a while, the incipient "Yuch!" went unuttered; beauty came to the eye of the beholder. And such beauty it was. Those large, liquid eyes bore depth on depth of suffering. His soul was like a deep sea floor above which the lead measure dangles in the dark waters, falling short. . .

Had worked on the city transport all his life. Predicted accurately to me months ago, that the bus and subway strike wouldn't go through. With his ruined face and cloven throat he looked like a chicken the ax had gotten sideways, a badly aimed blow. Speech slurred, hard to get at times. But those eyes! Nothing unclear there!

Had a near sleepless night, after summoning energies to get me to the hospital, after so long a time. . . . What grief! And yet, it appears, a necessary grief, commanded by the empty beds, the creeping pallor and cold wandering of wits that always carries the same message: "goodbye, goodbye."

The one-eyed nonagenarian lasted exactly one week. Last Thursday I said my name. He said slowly, "Berrigan, Berrigan, that's a famous name." And again, "You know what's the trouble with me? I've got a fifty-year-old mind in a ninety-year-old body."

A Chinaman was in high fever a few weeks ago, all tubed up, incoherent, unresponding; now he's shakily on his feet, walked about the corridor by a brother newly arrived from Burma. You never know. . . . Our most spectacular remission in fifteen months. Now Mr. Teng is to go home; people can hardly credit it.

Anton looks like Ramon Navarro playing *Tobacco Road*. He wears a magnificent silk robe with fur trim, stalks around muttering in French or Italian. Word is that he acted in *Casablanca;* but someone, straight-faced with devilry, made the mistake of mistaking him for a waiter in that film! That set loose a volley of foreign expletives. Then another comicotragedy—someone cut his hair too short for his taste. He lunged and spat, his chopping hand came down like a snickersnee on thin air, curses flaming from the bulging eyes. It is all like a forties movie, out of cycle, mock heroic.

Here's an urban ascetic. A fine face, pallid, bony; no coverup, no fat. Strong torso and arms; everything from waist down like a hanging appendage, an afterthought.

He hauls himself about in the bed like a seal on a rock, help of a steel bar overhead.

But his smile never fails, determined, a steely gaze. . . .

How attached I grow to the "new arrivals." They creep into your heart, these damaged bodies, a beggar's opera, a procession out of Bosch or Bunuel. They scrawl in the dust a history that the seducing illusions of youth and health and sexual prowess would like to erase. Suffering, death, corruption before death; the culture stops here.

I'm by no means the only one so caught up in this haunting beauty, this truth beyond bearing. Thursday Jim was getting his usual enema. They finished and he simply collapsed, as though his strings had been cut. Zing! He fell back, the puppet show all but over.

And sister said to me sorrowfully, "I'm afraid it's an embolism; if it is, he's a goner."

She couldn't have taken it harder if a healthy child were going under.

But the news is good, he came back from the verge.

For a time. It's always for a time.

I watch the sisters and orderlies in action; feel like Walt Whitman, all spectator, all eyes. Catholics, I think, are people who are freer to go crazy than practically anyone I know.

That doesn't mean, alas, that they normally embrace their vocation! We were told in the old days to "embrace our vocation." I said "free to."

The road unrolls, the first roadrunner goes on ahead, just

barely in sight. We have seen someone of whom it can be said, "He went further than any of us." But then we add under our breath, half-ashamed and with a covert look around, "But not further than we're invited to!"

An old man deaf as a wall, gremlin grin, face wrinkled like water under a spanking breeze. He sits there by the hour, knitting a white scarf. I shout in his ear, "What fine work you do!" He cackles like the goose that's laid the ultimate egg, "It'll keep someone warm when I'm gone, won't it!" I wrap the scarf around his head, hug him tight; he squirms with delight like the brother of Sister Fate. How to go!

Chapter 2

"BEFITTING"
A Poem

To speak of befitting   it would be more fitting by far
to enter on hands and knees   More fitting
to come in blind as the windows
petrified like the walls
more fitting to roll in like an old wheel
spun through the door by kids on the project
to come in in a wheelchair
hearing the front door   close like a last sigh
More fitting to enter like a dream walker
drugged to his ears   who sees in mad visions
(the unbearable truth—)
monsters   chains   fangs—
SKULL CRUNCHER who bares the brain   leaving a clean hole
like a surgeon's saw   for the pulsing grey matter to stare out
NOSER   he plucks the smeller   last rose of summer
JAW his clients leer with lipless glee
then TUBULAR   he loves tripe

So   they grin   YOU MADE IT THIS TIME
WE'LL BE BACK AT MIDNIGHT   WHEN THE DARK STALKER COMES
AND SNAPS OUR CHAINS

What they don't know
hurts nobody   They don't know
when they've had their fill of you
and gone back in shadow   and fallen like stones
asleep   and claws and paws
bear them ponderously away away in dreams

43

They don't know
how befitting the white robe
the candle lighted by the sister of night
the beckoning
the rising   rising in shrouds   the wonder
of wondrous Jerusalem   rejoicing   rejoicing
Majestic   you go
past the dead chairs   the morgue
empty as mother hubbard's
cupboard   the dead beasts in shadow—

I believe this   like Simone Weil
append my reasons   I believe
because I believe   Like the pebble in my shoe
the dark mote in my eye   The one I can remove
by slight effort   the other is death
spitting in my eye. The one I do not remove
being irrational   The other
for the life of me
I cannot
So live with it
walk with it

Credo quia impossibile

If the resurrection of the body
were possible
we must disbelieve
It were the work of this world   we were gears and bolts
of the hinges of brute time

THREE WHO WENT IN STYLE
The King of Conundrums

Old Sulkey won't let you near him five minutes without placing an order. Even a kleenex pulled or a kleenex tossed away. The service in the hospital is, ordinarily speaking, extravagantly good. But Sulkey wants extras on the extras. "Hey, give meen a cegaret. Hey, dank you verra mutch" (by anticipation). "God bless, light it now!" "Hey, mine Fadder" (his old skinny face is like a ruined sunrise, all glare and glory and a bad day ahead). Or, with a grandiose wave of his phthisic hand, "Here's a real preesht for you!" (Thus bringing another patient into the act, making it hard to turn down the next request.) "God bless, half-cup coffee plees, sugar sure, cream, no thenk you. . ."

He's taken the measure of the world, made its measure his own, to wit: It's not what you are that counts, it's what you have to give. So what do you have to give—me, for example? Along with several others here, I think now and again with passion, why does the old boy have to push everyone around, why does he have to go on like a sick cat in a sack?

You get angry, you're amused, you laugh, you flare up. Which is to say he foxes you into his game; you've graduated to his hit list.

Oh can he eat, he wants seconds on everything. "Hey, get me an orange, peel it plees, make it sections, how can I eat it udderwise?" His hands make extravagant circles of helplessness.

This his wife comes in; she's wise to him, her indentured
servanthood is an elaborate mime, eyes raised like a diva's to
high heaven. She sails around the ward, dispensing the
goodies she's brought; ad-libs with brilliance, facing things,
shrugging them off. And he watches from the blankets, not
missing a trick, ferret face crouching, eyes on twenty-
four-hour alert.

Discomfiting, unsettling. Does a Jew ever let well enough
alone, does a Jew let death well enough alone?

A thought occurs. If God were an old Jew dying of
cancer, he'd quite possibly look like this one, yell like this
one, watch and wait like this one, demand plenary service
like this one. He'd go out like a peacock, tail flaming. He'd
hang on to a priest as if he owned him, talk five languages,
each with a foreign accent, harass you if the goods and
services of creation weren't at peak. Bow and scrape, bow
and scrape, don't you goys know who I am?

And what would God's wife look like? This one is wise as
the ages, wiser by a long shot than God; shaped like a
Manhattan culvert, four by four, roaring into town from
some mysterious watershed, brim full of unaccountable
juices. . . . She looks like someone who knows she looks
like God's widow. And she's seen the will and testament.
Therefore, she smiles.

They wheel Herb into the smoking room. He's not in a
wheelchair, but a wheeled bed, which is the next worst
thing to a bed, which is the next worst thing to a drawer in
the morgue. Herb is black, a fact which in this place takes
on an altogether special resonance.

The blacks, that is, offer a kind of background method to
the foreground method of going under. Silence against the
music, silence against the complaining, silence against the
stark ravers, asserters, weepers. They form an ambience,

their breathing and then their not breathing; an atmosphere, a veil, an empty stage, a nondecor. Pure, empty dawn, pure evening, pure night—the will that shows a way, while others caterwaul on the fences or whistle their way past the communal graveyard, or into it. I want to be precise; it is very hard to be so. I want to convey how certain people die who have a passionate stake in not dying; but who are stuck in a culture where the main business is death and the main enactment of the skill is dying badly. I mean badly.

But all this is philosophical wheel spinning, an overturned vehicle. It conveys little of what I see constantly here, something at opposites to the culture. A Model-T chugging valiantly along under its own steam, up hill and down dale. Herb gets wheeled in in midmorning for a smoke, several smokes if he can con them before lunch. His bed reminds me of those wheeled vehicles they used to trundle millionaires around in, like John D. Rockefeller the First, in the newsreels of the thirties and forties. All their crimes, cupidity, bodyguards, union busting, scab hiring, the dark underside of the great fortunes; then the helplessness and fury of old age, all concentrated and captive in the tucked blankets and visored caps and wrinkled, buzzard faces. On the boardwalk at Atlantic City, taking the sun in the Bahamas, in the estate gardens of Palm Beach, the headlines said, They didn't die, they lived on and on, like the Greek god who asked to live forever and forgot to ask for youth. And so grew old—forever.

Their money brought them a bogus immortality, envy gathered around them, a cloud of flies. They were pushed and pummeled into life every morning by nurses and therapists; then they were strapped upright into the wheeled beds to meet the dawn, to meet the sunlight, to meet the press. . .

Here comes Herb on his bed. Sorry, there's no press.
And it's April in New York, there's no sunlight. We edge
his wheels in next to Sulkey.

And here, let us pause to observe these two, the old
black, the older Jew, the parryings, feints, conundrums—
and an outcome full of surprise. To Sulkey, the ebon wedge
of bone and brawn next to him is not much more than a
point of reference, as described above, a speechless opposite
number, the stare of two discomfiting eyes straight ahead,
as though a zero had turned on its pivot until it looked you
in the face, but disappeared in so turning.

Sulkey thinks Herb doesn't think at all. That's putting
the matter at its crudest, a matter as diverse as two ways of
dying—black and white. Sulkey despises Herb. Herb, con-
trary to all surmise, knows he's contemned, thumbed at,
talked about, much as though he weren't there. Hanging
around the two of them as I do, I'm tempted to think: What
a smartass on my right (no disrespect), what a dimwit on
my left. One dies with a screech, a claw bared; the other
merely goes under, one puff and he's out, dim, dimmer,
and done.

But not so fast. Last Thursday the following occurred.

Midday meal was over, Sulkey was wheeled from the
smoking room back to the ward to welcome Madame God.
Herb stayed on, having, as usual, no one to welcome. An
orderly took out a cigarette and sat down; Herb wasn't
really there.

Now the prevailing opinion around the place favors Sul-
key. Herb is a pleasant unresponsive dunce, Sulkey is a
very paradigm of stimuli, a pisser of some considerable
skill. In the face of which error, this monologue ensued. I
swear it.

It started with an offer. "Want a cigarette, Herb?" The
orderly held one out.

"Shure. Light it for me." Which he did. Herb puffed away reflectively, the smoke went in and out and up, slowly. Then a switch was thrown. Herb spoke up, no preliminary, no provoking.

"You know, that Sulkey, he's fulla shit." It was thunder in a clear sky. We sat up. It was as though Herb the dying stood up in his bones and stalked away.

He didn't. He just lay there, went on talking, slow as ever. "Yeh he's fulla shit. He saze thank you thank you when you er I'd say no moren plees. He think he can con you, he think you'n me dumb.

"You know he's fulla shit like a Chrismus turkey."

By now we were rolling on the floor. It wasn't just that Herb had suddenly busted his gasket, a talking binge. It was something more; he was turning the tables on our neat scheme of things. Who was the dummy, who the smartass? Who was calling the shots on whom?

"That Sulkey say God bless you God bless you. He don care bout God er you er the gatepost. He want you movin' this er that—for him! You know what?" He gestured grandly, the ash fell all over him. "I could take his pants down, sell his ass for turkey parts, thass what."

Another morning. My old monologist greets me. He squats on the edge of his bed, skinny legs off the floor, looking out on the world like a bright, green frog in a quandary.

Depending on his downer or upper mood, I'm treated to a diatribe against the follies of existence or a short treatise in praise of the grandeur of God. Last week it was the former, this week God is habilitated. He asks me what I do for a living. I grope about for a hook to hang life on, answer a bit dubiously, "I'm a teacher." "Of what?" "Literature." A long nod of the pate, to take in and approve such momentous news. Was there ever a Jew in the world who wouldn't tip his yarmulka to a professor, even one of rumor or mere self-assertion?

He seems confused enough, or secular enough, that the Catholic paraphernalia of the place entirely passes him by. He looks out at the statues and crosses somewhat as he looks at the people, equally remote from his gathering struggle with the Top Ikon of them all.

Oh in that hour, may someone meet him agate eye to eye, may all services be fittingly rendered forever. May the Lord of Isaac and Jacob (no ikon but friend and brother) greet his fragile, fierce counterpart, seat him at table, as Abraham seated the angels, and knew them not. And knows them, and Sulkey, forever.

Pete and the Art of Dying

Pete's voice: an iron wheel growling over gravel. Pete: a Polski on whose chest hangs that emblem of long and faithful service underground, the Order of Black Lung.

He was a man built like a mountain. He came in, a bull strapped to a wheelchair. People learned fast to take the long way round him. Pete flailed out against all comers, in all directions. His antic ways, known in the skull trade as "psychotic episodes," seemed to me something far different: an instance of hypersanity, rebelling against a fate that put the bull of the pampas in such a governable and humiliating harness.

Stuck, stuck, stuck. Sister told me that, one day, Pete reached out where she stood and simply picked her up. Ravaged as he was, he had sufficient leverage from the wheelchair to lift her off the floor and throw her bodily against the near wall, "like a small piece of furniture," she described it. It was sudden and frightening, a flash of genuine frenzy against death and his minions.

But by the time she recalled the moment, the edge was gone from her fright. She spoke quite dispassionately of "moments that simply have to be gone through, given a temperament like Pete's. He's always been active, a great worker; and here he sits—or lies. It's too much for him at times."

But Pete wasn't in the hospital for treatment of black lung. He bore a surface cancer the size of his great fist flowering in his groin. Pete's raging vitality fed and fed the parasite; and for the space of months, the same vitality kept him fighting, futilely as we knew and were sure he knew. But fighting nonetheless, with the blind instinct of nature itself. It never seemed to me that he minded dying, but his body fought and fought, a living animal half in and half out of the jaws of a carnivore.

He was a mild complainer, halfway between the saints and the hellions. But because he was stone deaf and, in consequence, spoke on a kind of slurred single note, nobody found him much of a rebel from the common life. One day his jaws ached, on another the New York air made breathing a heavy pain. Hem and haw. We heard it all.

Then his slow slide downhill got underway; less time on wheels, more in bed. His food intake went from prodigious to so-so to paltry. He had less to say, and said it with greater effort. And now, when you leaned over the bed, it was as though you stood over the open grave of a ripe corpse. Frequent dressings and cleaning and changes of clothing hardly helped at all. Pete was literally rotting to death before his death.

This big hunk of a Pole, he had so little to commend him. He was never attractive or popular, his deafness put him at distance, made him remote and intractable. So big a frame, he seemed perpetually at odds with fate, like a great beast driven to distraction by gnats. The broad plane of his face was flat as a canvas; he looked in turn blank or puzzled or vaguely discomfited, as though one dim life could both complain and forget the cause of its complaint.

And to die that way! In Pete's last days, death, which we commonly choose to personify, had neither visage nor form, carried no scales or scythe, was skilled neither in dance nor mime nor hot pursuit. Death was a gambler's disembodied fist, come down like blurred lightning on a winning card. Death held fast; he was winner. He announced his conquest by the most sickening and cowardly of means. He leaned close, he laughed in our faces from his carious mouth. Simply, we had forgotten the stench of death.

What did it mean? Had one of our senses atrophied?

Pete quickened that sense to life again. He lay there, carven, wooden, patient as a log, alive and stinking, reeking with the truth. Did life smell too sweet to be true, a big olfactory lie? Were we captive among the flowers, was the Big Embalmer approaching with his sweet talk, his needle, to plunge it deep, deep, to the joining place of marrow and spirit, to make of us his chemical darlings, his amortized, smiling, odorless tribe?

Pete lay there, an illustration from an old devotional text; Bona Mors, the art of dying well. . .

We were once advised, in a dusty tome whose sentiment and symbols bore our grandparents and their parents aloft on wings of eagles, to a place of "refreshment, light and peace"—instructed that Christians "strive to imagine with the interior senses, the odor of our ancient enemy, worse than the stench of a rotting corpse. And thus to derive from this spiritual exercise, such horror of sin as will allow us in that dread hour, gracious access to our Saviour."

Papa Oscar and the Terminal Stakes

Swear it, Papa Oscar's winning the equine event called Terminal Stakes. Hands down, fierce odds despite.

He pads about in a wheelchair like a web-footed creature, grounded, ungraceful, but ultimately efficient. In the slowed world of the hospital, where any form of self-propelling is a victory, what to call him? I call him winner. . .

No swan song for Oscar.

The image persists: feathers, feet, appetite.

Oscar, that is, steals like a raven. He came here in virtue of a straightforward medical decision: to die. He lives on, to steal. He steals every day. Every day he steals something.

But first, to the question of language. What language do you talk when you command two—Spanish and English—when, moreover, you lie at the mercy of Anglo mercy? Oscar refuses to speak English.

To meet him you might say, ignorant of the governing subtleties. "Here is a round-faced old seraphic Hispanic in a bad fix. He understands very little of what goes on around him; he is charming in a rather defeated way." Ignorance is bliss, your ignorance. You might even pity him, never knowing that your pity granted him a crucial lead in the home stretch.

Pity? Now Oscar has a circle of freedom in which to move, to con—you and death and whatever unidentified flying object comes his way; electric shavers, crucifixes, watches, rings; yes and bananas and apples and icebox contents passim; also paper clips and cup of "coffe black con mucho sucre."

Keep your eyes peeled, especially your third one. Something is being acted out here, something momentous, a dramatic seizure of life, hour by hour, day by week. . .

We don't need "life" in the abstract; we merely want to live, another matter entirely. Papa Oscar wants to live; therefore he plays at thief, utterly detached from personal possessions, grandly liberal toward others. Behold, a wonder. What is superfluous to one's self becomes both heart's ornament and largesse, windfall.

And what of the ill-gotten goods? Gleaning without tremor or second thought, even from dying hands, Oscar stashes his take in this or that odd pocket of the place. He's like a chipmunk or raven or squirrel. Winter's ahead; so what else is new, it's always wintry for the dying.

He'll signal me over to his corner, reach into his store, bring out some perfectly useless, redundant trick or trifle, something you wouldn't burden your worst enemy with, a bottle of toxic shaving lotion, a noisome bar of soap. Wordlessly, with infinite earnestness, vast gesticulations, he urges its immediate concealment. I register amazement, gratitude, the look of a Third World waif clutching his first pair of shoes. And depart, both poorer and richer.

A second beneficiary, a nephew, visits him with regularity. This worthy also and invariably departs with a transparent look and a brown paper bag, bulky, containing an assortment of aforesaid objects, large, small, indifferent, valuable, worthless.

Unless sister intervenes. She intervenes, let it be understood, not to accuse, denounce, raise hell, trouble–make, invoke the law, or indulge any other approved conduct of inflamed property holders. Merely to restore the balance which Papa insists stubbornly on disrupting.

This character! No giving up his primal instinct. He's altruistic as the sun, the sea, the teeming cornucopia of the heart. His peaceable, crooked glance questions: Who needs anything? Commands: Give it all away!

Sister hoves in sight. Like sunrise to the moon, to sunset

like moonrise, a contrary rhythm. Or she's Dame Justice, pushing against this hilarious freebootery. The boot pushes back—freely. I like it.

And the game merits thought. It conceals, reveals, dramatizes, makes bearable, hearkens to, finally unmasks, the spirits that lurk in shadow, the appetite that makes mincemeat of us all—Oscar, sister, electric shavers, watches, wedding rings. You know it: death.

Oscar steals from the dying. This requires a quality of nerve that leaves me breathless, the moral equivalent of, say, a climb straight up the face of the World Trade Tower. See him, if you will, sneaking on rubber wheels into a cubicle; the curtains drawn seemly, the breath labored, the hour short. There, in the awesome space between one shudder and the next, Oscar extracts unto himself some trifle or not so trifle, lifting a limp hand or wrist to expedite matters, transferring hegemony of ring or watch unto himself. And wheeling out once more, spurious, pious, a corporal work of mercy on the lam.

Excuse a mere opinion. If Oscar is to be reproved, if words like *shocking, crass, thievery* are bandied about his head, let us proceed gingerly. Go slow. We are in presence of no run-of-the-mill rapscallion, no klepto locked into terminal larceny. Indeed, a sound understanding of this knight errant is hardly come by. It waits on friendship, his and my friendship. Oh, I am constrained to add, a certain tacky congruence of souls, his and mine. . .

Papa Oscar is dead; the truth he blithely kept hidden—a treasure in a field, a shaver under a mattress—must at last be revealed. I am, therefore, authorized to state that Papa Oscar, neither rascal nor klepto, is in fact a genuine, genetically rare, endangered, altogether unique avis, *oscariensa celestia,* roughly translated, twice-born antihero. Salvation is his. He now dwells in the company of others like himself:

Kierkegaard, Isadora Duncan, Kafka, Pirandello, Dunes-
berry, Emmet Kelly, and (in his best moments) Tom Mer-
ton.

All those, I mean, who never made it in this world,
indeed never wanted to. And were, rather, constantly in-
structed by a bony finger waving in their faces: Don't try.

No reason given, nothing trite like; it isn't worth it. (Who
needs fate to tell them that?) Nothing religious like; that
wouldn't be God's will. (Who needs religion to tell them
that?)

It was just a finger, as far from reason as it was from an
attached hand; explicit, inscrutable. It waved there, not
constantly, but zooming in as occasion required, pointing
out the needle's eye, the rocky road.

So they never made it. They not only didn't make it big,
they didn't make it little, not even miniscule.

With the finger in their faces, the question didn't even
seriously arise. The needle's eye, the rocky road! They
turned to other matters, matters generally neglected in the
big scramble for the wide gate, the mossy way. Matters
like, biblically speaking, the neighbor; artistically speaking,
the next *pas de deux*, the tying and untying of Greek knots;
humanly speaking, the next pilgrim over the hill. They
turned to these matters, turned, turned.

Their eternal ambiance is bizarre; I am authorized to
describe it. A flea circus, a waxworks crowded with images
of *their* heroes, a Bergman presbytery haunted by an anti-
pope, a zoo of tigers and wildcats in custody of mice and
moles, a monastery in shape of a keg of beer. Their vesture
is pied, their appetite for lager and limericks prodigious.
For a living, they fence watches, crucifixes and wedding
rings, cultivate groves of apples and oranges—and give
everything away.

But enough. I summon Oscar, a benign crooked spirit.

Let us pronounce a beatitude over him. Oh Oscar, blessed are the detractors, subtracters, invaders, sappers, of private property. Crash go the tables of the money grubbers. Whip, whip goes the whip. Clatter, whirr go the hooves and wings of the liberated beasts and birds. Blessed are you, Oscar, who wanted nothing and so set creation free.

That *rarissima avis*, he flew for years in the face of a phoney principality, kept that black bat wing off balance, off course; he derided that sinister being for whom practically all who dwell on earth show too much respect by far. Respect? I mean adoration, idolatry.

Who has named this inflated nonentity? Is it to be "property" or "death"?

Maybe the two are in fact one, a hyphenated horror?

Oscar pads away on his wheels, away, away. Over his shoulder, always in Spanish, offers, "Mira, now how about that?"

Chapter 4

THE CHILD

I

He came in here silent as the dead.

In the multiple skills of medicine, no promise is offered that he will ever speak again or hear again or see again.

Nor is there reason, in bloodline or friendship, to keep him alive as they do here, to care for him with such fervent love.

No reason why hearts should slow or heads shake from side to side when other patients pass his bed.

He came in as a stranger; he will die and be wheeled out exactly on that basis.

No one so young has lived so long with us.

No other patient stops us in our tracks in such a way, as though a passing bell sounded or a void opened under our feet.

You could imagine this or that conversation taking place with him, a bond of endearment. What would he say to us were he to speak? Would he weep, would he play some bedside game of checkers or chess or word building? Would his appetite be huge or lightsome? Would he show us one or another of those gestures, nods, smiles, frowns, plays and ploys that children use to try us, to make the world bearable, to make sense of us?

He has in fact only two or three changes of expression; they are sudden, clumsy as successive flashes in an old stereopticon. Only by a generous extension could they be called gestures at all. He lies to right or left like a supple doll, exactly as placed. Sometimes, when one grasps his hand or strokes his cheek, his eyelids flutter as though a

58

breeze had passed over his unsteady soul. And that is all.
I am trying to say that he has no claim on us, he has no
way to build a claim. How do you push a claim on the
living, when you hover so nearly out of life, when none of
the manifold gestures of the human dance is open to you,
any more than to the unborn, say, or the racked or the
drugged, or an outsider to the human predicament, a bird
or animal? How much we make of birds and animals! We
patronize them or collect them or eat them for dinner. They
are our ornament, distraction, counterpart, mime. But they
do not come very close. This child has come too close.

Because he never says a word, we can imagine him saying
anything, anything at all. Would he judge us, curse us out,
rain his anger on us. . . ? His silence is terrifying; it is like
the silence of God; it could mean anything, anything.

What do you do with a God who is silent? What do you
do when God says nothing, but closes lips and eyes and
turns his head aside and sleeps time away, your lifetime
away, and His? This child is terrifying, is an image of God.

They told us when we were children: You are made to
the image and likeness of God. But we so distort the image,
like a face in a pool of water when we toss a rock in. We
open our mouths, we distort the image of God. We stop the
mouth of God.

The silence of God. It can only be imagined. We open
the Book of Prophets, we think of his silence as wrath. And
how right we are, and how wrong. How wrathful God is,
yet how forgiving! The scourge of the faithless and
backsliding and violent; yet their mother too, their (our)
comforter and guardian spirit, advocate, the one who stands
firm even in a bad cause.

Is this dying child capable of wrath? It is almost unthink-
able. He lays abed like a cut flower or a fawn stricken by
arrows. How can he be angry ever again?

We think of God as endlessly fecund, the summit of the days of creation, doctor and instigator of process; the corn God, the one of endless frontiers, of space and time and black holes and quantum leaps.

Still He is God of modern life, who bids us to "come apart with me to a desert place." His mouth is parched. This God covers his face with his hands, as we up the ante on our cosmic roulette, concoct neutron bombs, make high art of duplicity and murder. This is the God of dry places and noonday devils and thirst and fasts and cancer and no outcome but death. "Where is He in all this?" we cry. He is asleep, mortally ill. He is blind and deaf and dumb to our crimes. Or so it seems.

Again, we think of God as master of judgment, infallible reader of hearts, He says to one, "Depart from me to everlasting fire"; to another, "Come blessed of my Father." We have read God right; He weighs our great crimes to a featherweight. He knows us as one knows sons and daughters, idolaters and killers.

Now, perhaps, we come closer to who God is. The child sleeps on, the child whose mortal illness is a judgment, the child who goes, first and innocent, into that other side (of which this side is the true other, in the sense of grotesque and malformed and estranged from the love that conquers all dualism, even our own, all sin and division, even our own).

The child lies there, a mild figure, a figure of judgment. Has he sinned? He has not sinned, except insofar as a child bears the stigma of our sin. His tender flesh is a *tabula rasa* upon which is written in the invisible script of death; one with us, one with the deathridden, one with the deathmongers. Flesh of our flesh, dust to dust.

We are coming closer to the truth of the dying child. He is godlike. He is godlike because he is bearing, without guilt, the burden of the guilty. He is dying of cancer before he has properly lived at all, in a world which is a very nest of cancer, whose main laboratories and research centers and "value-free" universities are big and bigger with the nest egg of death by cancer. Now they have hatched the infamy, it lets loose a wanton proliferation of teeming death, in bunkers and silos and submarines and air bases and factories. The four elements of creation are off limits; no, they are possessed, are in service to the gods of cancer. We will all shortly be missing persons, according to this mad scenario; obits, dead ones who tell no tales, the dead whose true God is dead, a casualty to the false gods who ape life and live off death, the false gods who are our true god.

But as to this child. He dramatizes before our gaze the fate of Jesus, which is to say, the fate of humankind. That fate, as we may read in the gospels (and in the face of this child), is ineluctably tragic; its highest form, the one furthest removed from the valid expectation of this world, from all cultural con jobs and secular folderol—that fate is to be a victim.

This is the scandal of God. To create here and there, and rarely and now and then—and sometimes by the millions in our hideous holocaust-ridden century—to create godlike images, victims, the innocent, those whose lives go before the universal fact of death, those who illustrate the common fate, for whom nothing is assuaged or put off, nothing screened or prettified or made cosmetic. Nothing but. Nothing but death. No hope for such. Nothing of skill, of science, of the fact or myth of genius, can turn this fate around. Nothing avails, no one intervenes.

These are the perfect form of things. Or rather (we had best be modest on such painful ground), these are the least imperfect form of things. The dying child is the least imperfect form of our destiny. Far less imperfect than ourselves. Guiltless, yet his death is consequential on guilt. Godlike (and here it seems to me we touch the face of truth) because he bears the consequences, anticipates the hideous death sentence, dies by the cancer of the laboratories, the cancer of the bunkers, the submarines, the SAC bombers. All weapons have converged on him; their target is children. They are accurate, we are told, formerly to the mile, now to the foot, the inch. They discharged their horrors, the child fell, he lies here.

When they asked me twelve years ago in the Baltimore courtroom why I went to Cantonsville to burn draft files, I said, "Because I did not want the children of the judge and the jury to die by fire." The judge pounded his gavel furiously. "You cannot come up months later with motives you cannot have had at the time of your action," he shouted. How could I help him understand?

If someone is to bear the high dignity of the godlike child, he or she must have a knowledge that goes before the tragedy, as well as a spirit apt to receive its consequences. This is what it means to be godlike. It is not enough to know, one must be chosen to know. The first is mere expertise or hunch, but the second is a bitter vocation. Nor is it enough to suffer, for suffering, as we see all about us, is as apt to "make a stone of the heart." No, one must be chosen to suffer, and thereupon choose to suffer.

The little boy sleeps on. You see, he is like God, totally uncommunicative. He is godlike, he says nothing. Or, if his silence says something, I do not know what it is. But the burden of discovery is on us.

II

The story of this life! You have to construct it out of your head; a veritable fairy tale. No other way. He has no other life than the one I invent for him. . .

Once upon a time there was a little boy.

This child has no history. He is like an artifact turned out of a kiln only yesterday, a found object washed up by tide, something run over and over, flattened in the street. He was barely ten years old, barely a child, barely on his feet—and he was cut down, abandoned, lost. Cut down, as they say, in his flower. The time had barely arrived when he could say, "Once upon a time," could tell a story for children; and now the story must be fabricated about him if, indeed, his life is to have any story at all, any movement, any hand-me-down to us.

If only I could start in somewhat this way, half in anger, half in humor: "Do you know what that kid said to me this morning? He said school was for the birds. He said he'd take the birds anytime over that old crow they call a teacher. He said, 'Couldn't we skip it and go to the Bronx Zoo and see the birds?' "

This outrageous kid doesn't exist; he has to be inferred, constructed. He does not exist. What exists is a shell of childhood, a coffin of a body, all but closed forever.

His day? It is unlike any child's in the world. His day is like the day of any dying patient. Dying; patient. He could be of any age, twenty-five to eighty-five. What is very nearly unbearable is that he is ten. He is washed, fed directly in his veins, diapered and changed, wheeled about in a bath chair. Irrespective; the care is personal as it can be, impersonal as it must be. There is another day to be gotten through, not necessarily a bad or good day; its signal arises out of nature, out of sunrise, out of hunger, out of the clocks' faces on the wall. Change us, wash us, feed us. And now and then a slight flurry of sorrow and grasping and flailing about, the whish of closing curtains, the mysterious cry, the breath stopped in mid-breath. That, too, death on his brief willful rampage. No more fury or flurry than the capture and beheading of a barnyard chicken.

But as to the child, suppose the following. . .

Someone is showing in a darkened room a series of colored slides concerning a child's life. They are photos taken on a single day, in the country, on a picnic. The child is much in his element; there are food and family and other kids, all the racy chaos attendant on the release of young animals from their urban cage.

The slides bring back the day, the sweet cheat.

Then, without warning, something happens. The automatic slide changer goes awry. Now we see, too rapidly or too slowly, the same photo twice, the next one halfway across, the next upside down. Following those, a blank light on the wall. Another. Then someone smells burning. A voice yells, "Turn on the light someone, the damn machine's gone beserk!" Without warning, a blinding flash, a whoosh, a cloud of smoke. The lights go up, the slide machine and photos are a smoldering wreck. . .

This is not a story about photos of a life. This is a story about that life. Copies of the life, images of the life, cherished memories of the life—these are not what is being destroyed. The life is destroyed. That life is now awry, half in and half out of the world. The legs that kicked soccer goals with gusto lay like two parallel sticks on a woodpile. The life is a blank; there is nothing to show, to dodge, to embrace, to smile at, makes jokes with. Jokes? The child is enveloped in a shroud, a swaddling cloth, like an unborn butterfly. Jokes? No one laughs around the deathbed of a child; a scarf of awe floats outward from his body, envelops his mother, his brother, who solemnly stand there, place a statue and holy pictures and candles around the bed, around this ikon, this holy one.

His mother and brothers: solemn, close to tears. His mother holds his hand in hers, she smooths his hair, kisses his face, speaks his name. He is not dead, he is only three-quarters or seven-eighths dead. She longs to recoup, take up in her hands that vial of life. She cups his face in her hands like a wind-tortured flame. She cannot give him up, any more than she can draw him back to life, this all-but-drowned land creature she has borne into the world.

Then she gives up. The mother sets the child's head again, gently, on the pillow. She learns by such a gesture, week after week, the terribly shrinking boundaries of love.

Once she could work miracles; she brought this life into the world! It was easy, she boasted in her heart, exulting in her lovely son. It was easy (though it was hard, too, she smiled secretly). You made love, and nine months later, look! You had a son, you had a miracle, you had done the impossible, had scaled Everest, the future lay in your arms.

No, it didn't. Who said you had a son, who said miracles? Look here. See what I show you.

There is a skeleton standing by the bedside, an interloper, an undoer of illusion. The mother stands near her child, takes him in her arms, frantically or dreamily breathes into his mouth, croons to him, sways with him in an ecstasy of grief. And a bony hand interposes, separates the two rigorously, a mean spoiler, a nurse named death. "Please now," reproves the Big Jaw, "no scenes. You're disturbing the patient. And you're only distressing yourself. And anyway, visiting time is over."

A claw rests on the boy's pulse for a moment, replaces his hand under the covers, smooths the sheet, all with a proprietary air that plunges home to the mother's heart, a blade. Big bones, claw, feet planted there, burning sockets for eyes, that absurd cap topping all. Who owns the child? Its mother? Death?

"I'll see you out," says the Jaw. It's more command than invitation. The mother wilts. She gathers her belongings, looks long at the boy. Then she waddles out, feet like an overweight hen's, shoulders drooping, defeat written on her absurd hat, her sad fur piece, her sloppy hems. . .

But I am not the boy's mother. I am not a welfare victim; death over me has no dominion. I watch that chalky abomination showing the mother the door. An owner, a dog.

I go up to the bed, hot with anger.

The skinny shinbone has his back to me, deliberately; he's doing something needless at the bed table. Without preliminaries:

"Why treat her like that? Doesn't she take enough abuse from life without getting it from you?"

He wheels around, this orderly of the death house, you can hear his bones screeching in their sockets.

"What's all this?" with a ferocious sneer. "You seem to forget, Father"—his voice curves upward, a mockery—"visiting hours are over; that goes for the clergy, too."

I look him over, slowly. An arrogant flight of fancy. White on white. If his eyes weren't now and again shooting fire at me, he'd be all but invisible against the white wall. And he takes me on, with a vengeance.

"Tell me, Father, have you blessed the little one lately? Your healing powers are sorely needed here, as you must see. Alas, up to the present, our little patient seems no better for your august presence. Or perhaps you've exhausted your charisms, you've come to our little casualty quite worn down in soulful capacity?"

I stand there, shamed. In all the weeks and months I had come and gone, I had not once thought of myself as a healing entity. Priests come in, chaplains come and go, they make enough crosses on the air to people a graveyard with markers. And what do I recall? Once or twice, a dying Irishman, a blessing asked and given, that was all.

He read it in my eyes, no contest; he was sharper than a

serpent's tooth. Head to one side, he took another tack, small fun; this two-bit priest, cut him down to size.

He waved a hand in my face. "Oh, but don't let me disconcert you, no offense intended. Granted, your magic has gone flat, no cymbals rattling in the wards. But then again, very little is clear today, is it? Priesthood isn't clear, no clear lines, virtue, vice. So many subjective juices in the air, steamy feelings, contrary voices. . ."

His voice was dry and hard, his finger poking the air. "You work your side of the street, Father, I'll work mine. But don't cross me." What passed for a hand shot out of his sleeve like a knob on a club. "Go ahead," he hissed. "Run for your holy water, buckets of it. Push the crucifix in my face. Once upon a time you'd have me screaming backward, diving out the nearest window. No more no more no more." He sang the words out in three keys: high, low, and horrible.

You knew he was right, knew he was wrong. Right or wrong, he had the boy in his grip. That was the issue; was there any other? "Tell me, Father." His skull stood sideways on his neck, an art appraiser just before the hammer goes down, sold. "Tell me, are you afflicted from time to time with a sense that you're dying too?

"People like you, you rail on about a dying church, dying America. Why not say it? You're in the middle of this, up to your neck." He went on and on, a kind of relentless rant.

"Up to your neck. You're half-dead. You expect less and less of your life. Less of your sacrament, less of your two hands. Less consecrated bread, less forgiveness. You're careless as a whore of your body's powers. You come in here, run for the buckets, the coffee cups, the trays; rush about, dour, hard hit by life.

"Come now, Father, what are you running from, where's the good outcome? How about a little examen of conscience? How about all those unmortified days and nights, the despair, the giving up on others?"

He was shaking my soul, a leaf in a mad wind. Something of the truth, a partial truth, coming at me straightfaced, a spurious judge, the demonic playing God; that mean and demeaning underside of the truth, that slug in the shadow of the living leaf. I raised my hand, wordless, appalled. My hand turned over, I half-expected to see on its underside some crawling horror.

"You lie, you lie in your teeth," I cried out.

Then I breathed deep, made my move; went past him, or through him, that bat out of hell. I took him with me at a rush, his voice trailed off, a bat squeak muffled in web,

took him with me like a veil of mist, like tears, my own tears
and swept him away, that mummy of death
and bent over the bed and took the child in my arms, lax, breathing,
insolvent, somniac.

And the child spoke to my soul:

"Believe me, friend, I know why you come here, and I thank you for it. I cannot say it, but I know. Soon you will awaken as I will awaken, on the other side of this illness, this burden. And you will ask, 'Did I dream it all?' No, you did not. Tell the world, tell your own soul, no, you did not."

He began to chant, it was like a keening, but the words were not mournful, they were exigent and plain and familiar. "Blessed," he cried in a high atonal whine, like the chant of a muezzin. "Blessed are the peacemakers, they are God's children." And his head fell back.

III

I wanted to come to his bedside like a fussy parent, shake him soundly. Come on slugabed, get up! Why all this sleep, sleep for food, sleep for drink, sleep for sleep—get up!

Listen (I'd be shameless, I'd strike a bargain with him). If you open your eyes and do me an immeasurable favor, a mere look in my direction, a favor I assure you I would value beyond say all the peerless trash in a Tiffany window. . .

If, little one, you will rise to your feet and struggle into your jeans and convey even a lick and a promise of water to that ineffable face—if, moreover, you will nudge your feet into your not-so-clean sneakers. . .

Why, I would take those so-ordinary instances of our common estate and fate as absolutely unique! Miraculous! Would rush out of the house to inform the astounded passersby that, yes, the boy within has arisen, is clothed, washed, and now stands poised on one toe, on the invisible tip of his five-pronged destiny. That there he flutters and turns like a star in orbit, awaiting the behest of the spheres, the divine order, the disposition of his day to wit. . .

And beyond doubt that throng of former strangers would take fire, would toss their caps in the air and utter a great cry; as though from a guarded Eden, amid thistles and drawn swords, had issued a great shout from the avenging angel at the gate: "No fall after all!"

Meantime, within the house, I came in to see what was transpiring as to our resuscitated darling (but never is such a word to be breathed in his fiery presence). He leaped from the starry pivot where he hung, unwobbling, only a foot or so off the ground, revolving like our own dear Adam, our Christ, our Juan—he leaped I say, into my arms. And I, scarcely crediting the evidence that pressed on me, the silkiest flesh breathing there, the warmth, the elbows and knees and arms—that congeries so shortly before, all but given over to the chalk caves of eternity and the floury keeper of the cave of sockets and dry mouths. . .

Now that dear unity, that delicious motion, watery, articulated, mysterious, from the subtle pulse of the wrist, like a butterfly under the skin, to the grand spasm of restlessness that cascaded through his limbs. . .

He would be off and away.

"*Where* is my world," he cried, "so long denied me, and I denied its ice and fire?"

Then he looked in my eyes steadily, bargainingly; "What will you give me, since I have cut loose from the cave and its keeper, who had promised me

if I would hold my breath and endure a little cold and run quickly uphill a long way

and never once look back. . .

—promised me that in the chalky caves I would own the doubloons of John Silver and the jewels of Ali Baba

—promised me that when we reached the cave and he and I had rolled a great white rock against its mouth

I should play there forever and have at my beck and call a sooty squad of minidemons

and so forget you forever

only

I could not—

and he lowered his head and was quiet—

Then he pushed hard on my chest and looked at me eye to eye, no longer crushed to my heart like a lover, but now my opposite, my adversary. . .

"What will you give me for all that? Since I said no to them all, and returned to you?"

"Let me show you," I said. And we went out-of-doors together. He groped for my hand and held it.

"As much of the world as is mine is yours," I said softly

at the doorway, "all yours." I spun around full circle, arms wide. And the sun turned to a Catherine wheel, diminishing, intensifying, a lode of light. It came out of the sky, like the sky itself, the light of the heavens. And the earth ascended to meet it, the earth spurned our feet, climbed up and up to where that intolerable light trembled. The light of the sun grew dense and earthly, the earth grew luminous, transfigured, the two were fused.

And a planet alight, a five-pointed star, came to rest on the head of the boy.

I saw this, and he did not.

He said, unconscious as the newborn to any but its milky world, and yet twitching at his harness:

"No school today, right? Can we go to the Bronx Zoo and see the birds?" He pulled at my hand like a hand on a rein. Go!

Chapter 5

THE IRISHMAN IN FINALITY ALLEY

That look of the dying, it goes through you like steel wire, drawn and drawn.

This Irish hellion, mid-thirties, sere as a June leaf in January; he looks at me.

"You know something, you're a sleeper."

"A sleeper—what's that?" I ask.

"You're a cat in the dark. . ."

There have been others, presentable ones, unsightly ones, hundreds of them. Most don't show their sores so visibly until just before the end. But he's gaping with them, he stinks to high heaven. You can't bend over him without getting a dose, his breath, the whiff of things to come.

That's to the northward. Approach him from the south, you get it from his guts, whence his arse has been cunningly transposed. There, the odor is that of an open privy; which in truth he has become.

Drugs, alcohol, street smarts, talk, talk, talk—the hot wind would wither the pages of a world encyclopedia. After a while, you're spinning with it, you forget to ask yourself: Is he sane or daffy? As in Nijinsky, the leap is all.

In his hands, a big Connemara rosary with stones of solid marble. The first day I met him, he was inconsolable; it'd gotten lost. They found it, finally, in his water jug and he went triumphantly wheeling around, rosary draped about his neck. It was like a rake's progress in purgatory.

Of course he knew the Nefarious Name.

"Berrigan! So you're the one!" His eyes flared up, a light from a cheap match.

I had no comment. He was so near evading all the silly laws and cops of this world; the difference between him and me was dissolving into a rueful last-ditch smile. Doesn't Paul name death a kind of snatchall? This was a character you wanted to hang around; to hear, not his last words, an unlikely idea. Indeed his talk created, sustained, his fiction. He would go on and on like the brook, all sound and sporadic sense. A fascination gripped you: that he was alive at all, talking at all, a flare in that rain- and fire-damaged dwelling, a gutted shack in high tide.

I see him yet: yellow, neglected teeth, lips thin, finely-drawn, colorless. A tongue passing over, faintly pink and dry, a tongue like crêpe paper. . . . And the eyes. When he was drugged to the cranium, one open eye rested on you, the rakish look of a pirate in port, or death on a holiday. Then the drugs wore off, and he lay there or sat there and stank and suffered and talked. Those were the good times.

He had been in and out of mental hospitals, in and out of jails, in and out of cheap rooms on the Lower East Side, in and out of the church. His life was a revolving door, inject and eject; half of hell was getting there. Toward the end, after his colostomy and drugs and drunks, in and out, off and on, his mother showed him the door: "Get out and stay out." He could come for a meal, but as for her house (by all reports, no prize), the welcome mat was pulled in after sunset.

He took to the streets again, staggered into a final heap, was picked up in pieces. And over the hill to the cancer ward. . .

Mainly, the dying are wrapped like a chrysalis in the silence before the journey. I don't mean coma, but an intense musing, a withdrawal enforced by pain or entered by

choice. Frequently, the inarticulate life of the poor, espe-
cially the Irish poor, brings them to a speechless end. Most
are unable to tell the world, with any verve or art or self-
mockery, who they are, where they are, why they get
stuck. There they sit in the guts of the great cities, thrown
objects, Stonehenge people. They make the appointed
rounds, seldom probe or scream out at life's fury or injus-
tice or folly. The church doesn't encourage such deviance;
few of the first-generation Irish have an education that pays
off; only that early, grubby grind, long hours, short re-
ward, big on punishment, all to get the young inured to the
slummy future.

One day his mother appeared in the ward. She was broad
of face and foot as he was emaciated; ruddy where he was
white as a wall. She sat there silent and talkative by turns,
his turns; he interrupting at any and all points, no rules or
courtesies to govern his wildfire. He pushed in, a heap of
nonsequiturs, tacky or high on whatever pills had gone
down that hour. A word of hers would set him off, a high-
flying brain in search of anchor or outlet. It was pitiful, it
was brilliant. As if all those mad, wayward years on the
streets, shooting up in back rooms and toilets, studying
photography and Chinese painting, reading and whoring
and drinking like the throat of hell—all that storehouse of
degradation and spoiled glory were erupting, filling the
room with the stink of damnation.

And something more. This Irishman, condemned by
swinish choices, was also hooked on God; surely as a foolish
fish, gaping, dying in mid-air. There he crouched in Final-
ity Alley, rank breath, a past of no note, cancer for his
portion, a mouth like the inside of a sandbag, Mother Ire-
land and Mother Church and Mother Brooklyn mocking his
fair beginnings. And those beads. A Connemara rosary
clutched like a tough fishline, two hands pocked with grave

marks, white and brown, the stigmata of the long dying. Those beads! That ignorant ululation, no better (say the liturgical skulls) than a litany in Hindi or Urdu yelled out by pagans. Those beads told by mouths that knew no better, symbol of inferior art and dank churches and overheated pubs and bad food and overbearing priests and sporadic violence. How it all comes to roost, the world's frown like a cloud over the island of no snakes, the snake pit of superstition and woe, the hands that clutch the dead past and refuse the only present, that hang on to the rosary, die with it, are waked with it, buried with it, and (to come back to this ward and this unlikely phiz) cling to it, hell and high water.

He said to me again and again, "Help me believe, help me in my despair."

And I, "But you do believe, you took communion this morning."

"But anyone can take communion," he cried. "Help me believe."

And having led me that deep, into that seam of darkness, he stalled there, and I beside him, a rock wall against our faces, nowhere to go.

And I who confess to knowing little, and day by day lose ground on that little, at such moments I had nothing to say. And so said nothing, but held his hand in mine.

He sensed it, he was savvy with that still insight of the near dead; were not he and I, after all, in a like predicament? Which is to say, I knew as well as he that anyone, willy nilly, believe or contemn, love or be lukewarm, any publican or pharisee or freeloader in the world, could step up and take the Lord's body. And who was to say him nay, who was to forbid or read aloud the shocking indictment of craven hearts? He knew and I knew, he took communion that morning and so did I; who was to say whether we

received to our glory or damnation? Who indeed but the
Lord of the loaf, that one so skilled in the breaking of
bodies, in discerning the spirits, in reading the crooked
texts of lives?

So we gained a bit; a fraternity of sorts, a human basis.
That was what he wanted, not to go off alone. He had
enough of being alone, of the common way of life in the
world, make it or go under, dog eat dog, die of your heart's
refusals, failures; all of which, it must be insisted, was the
sum of his own choices, long and foolishly pursued.

Pursued, to this day. He knew what he was choosing. It
could not be doubted he knew. He knew it from childhood
and first communion and parochial school. That was the
trouble, as the trouble grew. You knew your choices. The
knowledge was weakness and strength, though among those
who stood over the young, elders and teachers and priests,
it was presented only as strength. ("You'll always know
what you're doing," they'd say, with a look that would turn
Mary Magdalen to a pillar of salt. "You know what you're
doing; further, the Blessed Virgin knows what you're doing
and Saint Joseph and your guardian angel and all the saints
in the heavenly court. . .")

They missed something. Having all those witnesses, hav-
ing them presented as hostile witnesses, as witnesses who,
like their mouthpieces on earth, always expected the
worst—all those eyes and ears ended up precipitating the
worst. Many of us, like my dying cohort, were led to expect
only the worst. We were led to expect, moreover, that all
those thousands of pearly, impersonal orbs bent on us saw
only the direst of outcomes; which is to say, surveying as
they did the course and outcome of human nature, and
shaking their heads at the sight, "How long a purgatory for
this one!"

It was like living your life out—all its seams and patches,

its amatory and biological details—in a hall of mirrors, the
other side of which was starred with seeing-eye angels. Or,
worse yet, being shoved onstage in a public theater, the
gallery crowded with one's maiden aunts, defunct and
dynastic . . .

So here at land's end sit the three of us—mother, son,
and myself—three formal unmoving figures in a pointilism
painting entitled "Land's End." He sips ma's egg nog, I tell
a story. Of how we once found in our attic, after our par-
ents' death, letters from my great-uncle Will Doherty. How
the letters urged my father, uncles, and aunts to leave the
farm: "There's no future for you there. Get your education
one by one. The first to leave, upon graduating, should
sacrifice and send back the help required by the next of age.
So that all may emerge into a better life." How Will was a
mere plowboy who decided at age twenty-eight, with no
Latin and less Greek, to become a priest. So, enrolled in the
Albany, New York, seminary, achieved some Latin and
less Greek, and was duly ordained. And lived only four
more years, to build his own church, to be struck one day
by a falling plank, to die in his thirties of something vaguely
described as a "lesion of the spine," to be buried, finally, at
Whitney's Point, New York.

Luck of the Irish? The mother sat there, turned to stone.
She cried out against the curse. Her life, her life, "cleaning
the apartments of her betters," working in the parish
cafeteria for less than that legal dole, a "living wage." It was
unfair, unfair. Her burdened body planted, going nowhere,
like her life, she keened away. . . . "The Irish don't stick
together like those others." (A circumlocution, as we knew,
for you know who.)

But when gossip or memory touched a nerve, her eyes
sharpened like knives. There it was: the skill, the unsheath-
ing of the blade, the power of memory which is terrible and

vivid—and so seldom life-giving. You could hear it hum-
ming away in the great cities, where the Irish borrow the
survival tactics (of you know who), settle into ghettos,
trample the past, make mincemeat of the future. She
wanted to fold her hands, forever if possible, run like a
banshee through the labyrinth of the past, where all the
defeats and glories of the Irish are stored, emblazoned, em-
balmed, and now and again confound the world by rising
like Christ on a shield of legend.

"Oh, we were something!" she turned to her son.

"Your father was a Maynooth man, holy to the end. I'd
come on him at night, on his knees by the bed; an hour
later, there he'd be, on his knees, asleep at his prayers.

"But what did he make of his life? Seminary, two months
away from priesthood.

"And he blew it all. Landed in New York in '27, to end
up a window washer. Washing windows! A bare living, no
life at all."

She lifted her red hands, widespread, thick as a man's.
"All that toil, that promise!" A hospital ward, a wastrel son
beside, her man long dead, her boy sliding downhill to the
end.

Abruptly he turned away from her, his green eyes rested
on me, wide open. The drug was wearing off, the world
was nudging him, a hot prod in the ribs.

"How about a cup of coffee?" He brought me back with a
snap; he could be sharp as a sarge presenting arms. Wasn't
it, after all, his show, not hers or mine? Who was dying
around here anyway? . . .

You can mix fact with fiction and call it heightened fact,
or something less grand. Depending on whether you're
Irish. You can mix faith and brute folly and call it living;
you can snatch faith from the jaws of faithless conduct; you
can whirl your Connemara beads overhead like the sword of

ghostly kings; you can briefly beguile time, stupefy the three-headed dog that guards the gate.

Good, bad, indifferent, you do what you can. When it comes down to it, you're no better than a botch, put together by fate and foolish putty and, here and there, a sound bolt and a working joint. When you suffer, you suffer badly. You live your purported life as though you were shinnying up a greased pole or tumbling down a fever chart. Which it may be, you are.

And then you come to die. And that's when the only thing that counts begins to count. Your last moments tick away, an unresponsive listening space, a silence called out sternly by the very old or the young who have died in this ward, in these beds. They signal for silence; they sweep aside the hounds of death; they claim you head to foot, every failing inch. And your unteachable renegade heart misses its beat; you rise to meet them, the presence of something that, once and for all, makes sense, makes sense of it all.

Chapter 6

FOUR WHO WENT HARD
The Loser

This is the way they go. Various stages, tics, reprisals, angers (rare), silences, raunchy humor; many long, piercing looks; the sorrow of knowledge; moods of acceptance, holding back, yes at evening, no before dawn; tears and stony incapacity of tears; bedsides and wheelchairs unaccompanied, unvisited, stark, loved faces coming and coming back, to wait, to suffer through. . .

One of them, flat out, waxen, stentorian, chugging away on his back, a few hours remaining. And at the bedside, a daughter and her husband, "pass the time" playing poker. Seldom if ever do they look his way, never reach out to hold him, never speak to him.

Why are they there at all? Why did them come? A sorry parody of devotion. They are sober and intent; but only on their game, only for that.

Once dead, the father will be waked in tears, visited by a weeping throng, attended strenuously all day long by the black-clad pair, obedient to convention, conscious of onlookers, keeping the watch.

Now they play a different game. The living one is of no account. He can do as he pleases, breathe or stop breathing, linger or go; who cares? It is a terrible thing. The dying man is indifferent to the living, who are indifferent to him. But he can do no better, he has slipped his moorings, lost his way. His poor frame concentrates terribly on its next rasping, indrawn breath; his life is sucking in and out of his blue mouth, an infinite distance, darkness lies at the pit of the throat and beyond, beyond.

How fault him? For what? If he could, he would cry out, with the breath which hovers helplessly above a bottomless lake, "Please hold my hand, please speak to me, utter a prayer for me!"

If he were able! He would reach out imperiously, the hand that shudders on the counterpane as though laid on hot metal. He would reach out with angry purpose, scatter those mocking cards, would cry out, "You heartless fools, how you demean yourselves in despising me!"

The dying man cannot do this. He is done with being father to her, in the course of nature and the course of spirit. He has failed her, failed to convey the assumption, the outreach, the spontaneous sweetness, which might have returned to him at this hour, bread on the darkening waters.

He is done with being father, in the course of nature. And in the course of spirit (herein is the tragedy), she is done with being daughter to him. The first is a law of nature. The father is dying, he shortly will be father no longer. He is done commanding, beckoning, reproving. (But is that all there was to it?) This is the tragedy, that was all there was to it. So she is done with being his daughter, because that was all of it. He commanded, beckoned, reproved. But what did he fail to do? He failed to be father; so he fails now, when fatherhood has run its course, and death is running fast. He cannot be a friend.

She is no friend to him. Her face is stony, her blond head wary, set, attentive to the frivolous cards. She gives not a glance toward him, not a moment's attention to his last hour and its attendant pieties. She is there for one reason only, edgy and pointless; because the pressures of life are as heavy, as redundant, as enslaving, finally as stark mad, as the pressures of death.

She is here at his bedside; she will be there, a day later, beside his corpse. Someone dictates these things, somewhere, on tablets of stone. So she obeys, with a heart of stone, as she was once commanded, beckoned, reproved. He called it fathering, he called it living. What she called it will not be named here; but she dramatizes it with every slap of the cards, every metallic gesture of casting down, casting away, the disdain with which her eyes rest on, calculate, her life, her fate.

Look over her shoulder; she is a proud loser, her beauty is no indemnity against her fate, against fate's worse blow, which is called friendlessness. She has never won a hand, she never will.

Whom to pity more? I write this down, he is dead and buried. If her breath was slow and measured at his bedside as he lay dying, it was only to covet and store up breath against that great explosive sigh of relief she would loose when he was gone.

Relief, relief. For whom was death the greatest relief?

Failure, father?

The father is dead, a father and no friend. The daughter is, so to speak, living; but she is friendless, a failure.

The moral of all this is almost too sad to dwell on. And why, in any case, should a sad story require a moral, any more than a joyful one?

I will set it down anyway, for reminder. Dear children, death lives on, the horror of it, its humors, its bloodthirsty appetites, its feral hold on our throat. Unless, unless. We must cut free. Or better (for we have neither strength nor instrument to deal such a blow), we must be cut free.

And who will cut us free?

Was it out of such a sense, the sense of death not done with, never settled once and for all, that the vampire myths rose, the stories of the dead who stalk us, thirsty for our blood, making us pay and pay?

Unless Someone intervenes.

And Jesus cried out in a loud voice, "It is achieved."
And we were cut free.

Jerry: Anger and Aftermath

Here's to Jerry who's going out hard.

I noticed the changes over the months. It struck me one week, he's not walking about anymore. Then, he's stopped talking; what is it he doesn't want to hear, want to say?

It seems too easy in such cases to shrug, "Well, they have the right after all to go their own way. . . ."

In fact there isn't any "their way," any more than there's a "my way." This ought to be true of dying as well as living.

I went to the sister for some light, after spending a long time with Jerry, trying to coax a few words out of him, about him. Sister: "You'll be glad to know, the other night he blew his top. Yelled how awful it was, wrapped in a diaper like a child, no control anymore, dependent on everyone. Such anger," she went on, "could only be called a relief, a good thing." But where to go from here?

He languished, like all the others; yet something startling, something of himself, surviving too. A beautiful, direct gaze, a slight Polish blip to his tongue.

I went back, started over. Among other things, asked what did he fear, what was he fretting over, all those hours and days of utmost silence. . . . I was holding the hand he held out to me. . . . What was on his mind, would he give out with it?

He listened, brows knotted, all concentration. I began to sense something; it wasn't fear at all that was eating at him, but a boiling anger he had no vent for.

He said nothing, day and night he said nothing. Except for the courtesies, which didn't count: "Yes father, no

father, sure I'm OK, no thanks, no I don't feel like eating
anything. . . ." And all the while he kept staring over my
left shoulder. Not as though I weren't there, almost as
though someone else was . . .

First, I thought, comes purgation, that unanswerable law
of the land. Purgation first, free bed and board, hell on
earth, then. . .

Then one day he died, hard times to easy.

By all reports he quietly let go. His family was with him,
he managed a word or two. Then he girded his loins, took
up his bundle and went off alone, up and over Foggy Ridge.

And he left me uneasy, of two minds, his death gnawing
at the pit of my being. Where had all that anger gone? Why
had I been unable to help resolve it? Had the family helped?
Had anyone?

I thought about it, his dying that way, my sorrow a sense
of something raveled, something incomplete, as though an
uneasy spirit still walked the wards, shadowed me. Finally,
it came to me. Some hint, a closure, he and I brothers, a
sense beyond the blood, a sense yet to be realized. The
anger that boiled away in him alive in my soul. We two sons
of anger, fighting our fate to a last bitter round. In ways as
yet obscure, my life no more solved or resolved than his had
been.

So many missed chances, words unspoken. An illness
that left him bereft and broken, comfortless. And yet his
sorry days offering a measure of cold consolation—was not
his state of soul an image of the world? A world in which
most humans were as far from comfort or well being or true
peace as he?

Should have said. Could not find the words. Sat there
like a dumb animal, holding his hand, a communion unut-
terably bitter. Should have urged, "Embrace your anger,
warm your soul at its fires, nurture it like a living coal under
an icy sky."

My anger and his: an absolutely correct, blessedly exact response to a filthy state of affairs; since throughout the world large questions of justice and compassion stand neglected, ignored, since the poor falter and die unassuaged. But my litany is long as the trail of the wandering Jew, long as the dying of Christ.

His anger: that his last days reduced him to the humiliated condition of an infant. And above and beyond that, a crowning injustice: he, arbitrarily condemned to death, without ever being heard in the matter. . .

Dear friend, I longed to say (to this day I long to say) let our two angers join hands, knotted in one. Let the death of the innocent, the crimes of the rich and relentless, rage in our flesh; let the world hear our outcry. Let them know that we do not die without treading the fires of life.

Long live our anger, long as the fury of Amos—
They despise those who speak up for the right, they detest the ones who speak with integrity. Since you crush the weak and steal the fruits of their labor—these houses of proud stone which you have raised, you will never inhabit, those choice vines you have planted, never shall wine of them touch your lips. For I know how numberless are your crimes, how enormous your sin, you oppressors of the just, extortioners, you who crush the poor. . .

Long as the imprecations of the psalmist—
Let them be confounded and put to shame who hunt my soul;
Let them be brought to confusion who devise my hurt.
Let them be as chaff before the wind; let the angel of the Lord
pursue them.
May their way be dark and unsure;
Let destruction come on them unawares; let the net they have spread

take them captive; into that very destruction let them fall.
Let not my enemies wrongfully rejoice over me
For they speak no peace, they devise deceit against the
   meek.
Let them not say in their hearts, "So be it." Let them not
   say,
"We have swallowed him whole."
Long as the unquenchable anger of Jesus—
   Hypocrites, they preach but do not practice. They con-
      coct heavy burdens,
   intolerable, and lay them on human shoulders; but they
      themselves will
   not lighten them by the weight of a finger. They do
      everything to be
   seen by others, they love places of honor, the best
      seats. . . .
   Woe to you hypocrites, you shut the kingdom of heaven
      against others;
   you neither enter yourselves, nor allow others to do so.
   Woe to you blind guides, straining out a gnat and swal-
      lowing a camel.
   You whitened tombs, outwardly comely, full of bones
      and filth.
   You serpents, vipers, how will you escape being con-
      demned to hell?

And one day his anger died.
No one was around to catch his last sigh. It was the
classic American scene, too much followed by too little.
Bad way, good way, indifferent way? The clouds beetle
over us, the clouds scatter. Jerry's angry heart, a wound
where a heart should be, ceased its trouble. He went like
the rain that comes and goes, like rain and nothing else. His
anger cooled, his breath stopped short. On and then off like

rain, starting and stopping at its own sweet will. Like all those things we belittle or ignore or interfere with—weather, sun, rain, friendship, inconstant children, and meadow flowers, and the ring around the moon.

This is the way we come, the way we go; not, if we see things straight, inter feces et urinam; not in degradation; but reduced to the simple and natural, the vagrant and truthful. That is how we go if we are free to perceive it, don't put our blundering feet in the way of natural workings.

It was November outside. I thought, how apt it would be to celebrate Jerry's bitter victory. If his bed were left in place, and Jerry's big empty husk of a body were spread out on it. Such dignity, such a heart of silence! And then open the door and windows wide and everybody get out of the room (stop interfering) and let the winds carry Jerry off like a long flat light plantain leaf. Or if that's too much, at least let the lesser leaves pour in through the windows and lodge around Jerry's arms and feet and eyes like the start of a mulch under winter blasts. Let the leaves start the long, slow, flameless burning, decay, warm as a living breath stealing over that nondescript self-emptying of his. And let Jerry, a reborn child of mood and moment, join his subterranean cronies, minions, worms and bugs, to make of his still form an esplanade for the showing forth of the lowly glories of the creator.

But no. Not kosher. You could hear the superego, Big Boom the Intercom. *There are city laws for the disposition of the transmogrified dead!* Who, according to this theory and malpractice, have no will of their own, no collateral leanings toward the humble servants of time, the larvae and incandescent crawlers (who long, with every fiber, to feed off Jerry, empty him, carry him off on a flotilla of silken wings into the empyrean).

None of that. Jerry is hustled, with all deliberate speed, into the ice chest, feet first, there to await the ministries of Meeks and Saltpeter, Embalmers to Pharaoh.

And this I protest, this is a lowering of a high destiny. Jerry will be injected with purplish dye, varnished like a Dresden milkmaid. His face, round and golden as a turnip under a full moon, will be sown with peach fuzz. He will be sprayed with foul chemicals to ward off the ancestral spirits.

And those hands, those fans of his soul's fires, those gaunt beauties fashioned to mold the world anew, hands that signaled his resolute dignity as he lay dying (as once he lay making love, or sleeping, or holding a book at midnight); those hands that triumphed, in service, in intelligence, in the devisal of cunning artifacts—what have they done with his hands?

Unnaturally clean. Fingernails buffed like phoney pearls. No tools of a workman, a stubborn tiller of mind, a man marked by the world with its own grudging, admiring stigma. . .

Now his hands resemble a con man's or a banker's, those parasites of dollars and trash food, who die without remorse and clutch for all eternity the burden they once shifted to an army of slaves.

Where are Jerry's hands? Someone has stolen his hands, some necrophiliac artist longing to cast in stone or bronze these untoward relics of a vanishing tribe—the ideal, responsible, supple, interfering, musical instruments of creation, connivance, supplication, fury.

And then, and then, another sacrilege! That thief substituted in the dumb sleeves of the shroud a pair of mock hands. From some showroom window perhaps, hands suave as a hangman's cravat, hands neither calloused, misshapen, electric, persuasive, airy, inclusive, stern, sibiliant, snapping. . .

The scene is a Wisconsin TV station, whence I have been hustled to make small talk smaller. They purred at me sweetly, "Now before you go on the air, let's make you beautiful."

The hands hovered over, their rouges and scent, their ghastly nostrums. I stared into the mirror. Granted, not much of a phiz, but whose is it anyway? Whose tears are these, whose frowns, wrinkles, crags, whose mortality? . . .

Said, to the mirror, the tube, the image makers and breakers, the hands, their necrophiliac nostrums, "Over my dead body." Meant it, over my dead body. Saint Jerry, teach me to fend them off, the artificers of death.

The Greek Who Cracked the Code

A Greek arrived, smoking his lungs out. He could hardly draw his breath. He croaked at me in the smoking room, "Get me a cigarette, will you?" It seemed so foolish a request, to pull smoke in and out of his raw tubes, I protested, "You're breathing that hard and you want to smoke?" Back he came, no fooling around, "I'm dying anyway, why not?" I went for his cigarette.

The day before, he celebrated his fifty-fifth birthday. Just before the party he was running such a fever, he said to the sister, "Will I die today?" She took his pulse and temperature, then putting it all together, the longing in his eyes, the racing pulse and burning body, she said, "No, you're very ill but you're not dying; let's go on with the party." The party went on, the family poured in. That was Wednesday.

It's important to have the sequence straight. He arrived on Tuesday, the same week. Wednesday he had a party. Thursday he kept me talking most of the day. He died on Friday.

Salamagundi, born on Monday, died on Friday or so. The children's jingle is truer than we like to think. Or the psalmist's: All our lives are a shade, a shadow that passes.

You see it verified here, the foreshortening of life, the span of men and women no more than a hand's span, the cycle of moths or cactus flowers.

I remember Nick mainly because he didn't know the code. Or perhaps he knew it (I rather think he did), but lacked all respect for it, was determined in fact to crack it.

This is what I mean by the code, a simple matter, but austere; practically none of the dying want to talk about dying. They talk about their arthritis, about cold in the bones (!), about indigestion, about constipation; they have a thousand ways of saying, "Of course I'm ill, but not that ill. . . ." The code is the common, intricate web of understanding, looks, evasions, hints, fits, starts. It binds everyone. It says to the dying, in Morse or sign language or the body's tremor, recoil, embrace, "So the news is bad? You don't have to hear it yet, let's hold off a day or a month even . . . we can hold off as long as you wish, just give a signal."

They're like miners trapped a mile down. The message from them goes not, "Can you get us out?" (impossible, and they know it), but, "Are you still there?" (they know the mine by heart; they opened its seams, crawled its pitch dark, took their chance, lost).

Be there. It's medicine as art, the art of the possible, rigorously applied, without bounty or bargaining. Call it absurd; at least it's modest.

Here you can say (without saying it), "So you're going to die? Let's do what we can. . . . How about a whirlpool bath? Or a Scotch? Or a back rub?" Or, all else failing, "Will you stop *bugging* people? Do you think you're the only one in the history of humans to leave the world feet first?. . ." The thousand and one ways of making life and death bearable, or at least, less badly borne.

How did they concoct the code? Who did it? Where? When? Someone bends over, engages my left ear, the slightest, feathery touch. Whispers, "It all goes back to a vow."

Yes. What's going on here, on part of patients, orderlies, sisters, myself—we're working out our vow. But that's another story, what we vow, to whom, the way of it, the art of it. Let me say only, the way to crack the code is to submit to the discipline of the vow, its nuances, turns, hints, rigors.

But I'm getting ahead of myself. Nick the Greek smoked and talked. The time is roughly twenty-four hours before his death. Listening to Nick is like listening to a radio in a moving vehicle, in and out of tunnels. Nick fades and comes back, fades and comes back. You have to strain to get it, read lips and fill in.

What he was in a very agony to talk about was simply himself, himself dying. He was racing to the finish, he must get it all out. What a good life he had had! That was the burden of those last hours. What a good life! He would do it all over again, no hands, no feet! He would give up a hell of a lot of money and good health and making it in America, if only it could be the same wife, the same family, the same love. Love, that was all of life, all that kept things together, that made sense.

Only the day before, he'd called for the members of his family, who were, according to him, contentious and at odds. He told them solemnly, there in the hospital parlor, knee to knee and eye to eye, told them they must learn to love one another, they must try harder. It was everything, everything. They must believe this, it was the word of a dying man.

Now his hand was on my knee, the fever burning in his eyes, blinding. Could he see, could he see me? Whatever he saw, he saw more than this world.

His wife came in. She sat there at some distance from us, perhaps thinking we wanted to talk one to one. But when Nick grew passionate and that vehement, commanding croak took over in his burning frame, she got up quietly and, standing behind him, put her arms around him and held, held for dear life.

The Castaway Christ

One of the orderlies called me in to give a hand with this old suppurating sack of bones, Matthew, behind closed curtains. It's all but curtains for our friend, his bones squealing like the cogs of the last day.

Said Matthew came to us ten days ago, huddled up like a dustman's sack. He didn't want to live, didn't want to die. What else was there to do? They dumped him here in our dust heap; let him choose.

Behind the curtains Philip was swabbing him down. Poor Matthew was groaning now and then, a groan being all the signal he could send into the void—*not dead, not yet*. Philip, his face screwed up at the smelly mess, ruminated, "Five years ago, did I ever think I could take this? I used to gag at the smell of soap, a plain bar of soap. . . ." He kept rubbing and swabbing away, throwing the pads into a paper bag. We kept holding Matthew, naked as a new chick, legs and arms askew; he was like one of those badly assembled devil dolls they make to frighten children, tossed there on the bed, a childish fate.

A pillow stashed under elbow and knee, it was hard to tell his arms from his legs. Hard to call this poor castaway a human, to verify the human count—two arms, two legs, one torso, one head.

The head groaned, the castaway limbs lay there, lacking all that differentiated purpose which, without second thought, we assign to humans in motion.

This was slow motion indeed, or none at all. The only apparent move from Matthew was a heartbeat, that and the heartfelt groan. The latter could not have been more dismaying had it issued from a corpse. You do not expect the dead to groan; but neither, come to think, do you expect the dead to palpitate—which Matthew continued to do, somehow. It was like coming on a living body under a heap of the dead.

We turned him this way and that, we put his limbs in approximation to his frame. He was like a large, plucked turkey; his skin was filmy and pocked as though lately feathered. It had that dead-turkey quality: you could pinch it in your fingers, a ghastly, pearly white, cold to the touch, gathering at the joints in little wrinkles of nonlife. You all but asked yourself: How come the dead turkey lives?

I dwell on Matthew, stark emblem of mortality. We commonly love to take death on behind closed doors, genteelly, help of morticians and clergy, their death-denying smiles, crêpe drawn across their eyes, the press of papery hands—be comforted, the dollar lives.

Who takes death neat? The stirrup cup is invariably a mixed drink, aphrodisiac, soporific. Who takes it neat? An instantaneous flash, a voltage kick of mulish Christ. . .

Matthew's mouth is open, he breathes like a leaky bellows. The inside of his mouth is black, the smoke of human waste, a faulty flue. Not much left of Matthew. Every image that comes to mind suggests a death we would like to misbelieve or bypass or walk out on, help of mime, music, religion, subterfuge, art, pornography, guns and knives, luxurious musings drawn from the stoics or egoists.

At such moments we need silence, we need to summon great ghosts, to cast a scrim between our eyes and this puny

one, struggling like a butterfly on the rammed pin of fate.
Let Jesus break silence, since our poor words fail us, since
in our failure we betray or dismay the dying; Come you
blessed of my Father. . .

Everything around the bed is borrowed; who owns his
shroud? For Matthew, from the common cupboard, we
borrow a gown, clumsily push his plucked wings through
the sleeves. All he has, all he owns. Indeed, we are all he
has or owns. Now, let a dark muse, a ghost, hour after
hour, day and night, sit there at bedside, stitching the
words of Jesus on his shroud.

Misshapen Matthew, knowledgeable as an angel, silent as
stone. Mere days before his death he came to us, crouching
in the bed, a fetal darling. I met him there, reading from a
cheap ten-cent booklet, the stations of the cross. My eyes
took him in, lying on his side, knees drawn up, a stance I
thought temporary, an easement. Not at all. Matthew was
cast in stone, his muscles contracted like cat gut drawn,
tied. Of the hundreds of positions possible to a recumbent
body, Matthew had only this one. He was locked, minutely
calibrated, knees, elbows, chin, a geometry of death or
birth.

We exchanged, at that time, a sentence or two; he peered
at me out of his thick glasses, looking up from the text of
dying Jesus. Scarcely able to turn a page, turning to stone
before our eyes, the passion miming the passion, the goodly
dying, the gift.

Chapter 7

THE RIGHT HAND OF GOD

"So long, Fadda, get home safe. . ."

It was, as things turned out, something more than a conventional farewell.

I remember him, split-lipped, curmudgeonly, tough as iron nails, a found object off the Bowery; a fifth of Strawberry Blue, a filthy hand above the flood.

"Some of them are reeking when they come in," sister said; her addiction was to plain talk served up cool. "They come and come, ferried in by cops or public ambulances. In such cases, cancer is a byproduct of the Lono Swill, starvation, lowered resistance, no care."

Jack wore a cancer on his face like a rose held in his teeth. It bloomed there, a hellish transplant; his nose all but gone, overblown, an American beauty.

The sisters got him on his feet, spiritually speaking; and for a while, over a year in fact, physically as well. From slovenly he turned "picky," sister reported. With a gentle prod or two ("it was a lovely dying but a long one," she said, closing the ledger thereby with no tears), he began to consider the Four Last Things seriously, even with a sniffle of repentance. . .

He had a stash of money laid by. As was noted elsewhere, their rule forbids the sisters to accept payment for service. So they steered Jack to a local parish charity and Jack promptly handed over his sockful. He told me all this one day in a stage whisper, conspiratorial even in his virtue. . .

When the urban poor set out on the last mile, their bag-

gage includes few or no books. On the wards, they sit
blinking at daytime TV, a provender one would willingly
spare them. Jack became a fervent consumer. He had his
own chair and corner, off limits, secure as a pew in a parish.
There he slumped through four seasons, while the tube
spewed out its junk food, its spurious immortality, its
American boom and bust.

And outside, over the East River and the great steel hulk
of the Williamsburg Bridge, the sun rose for an emblem,
the seasons gave due notice, the south tending waters
mimed the mortality of the landlocked dying. . . . Snow on
the hardy trees, spring's first leaves; if you are dying (even if
you are not), the pageantry breaks your heart.

He turned his back: on nature, on the outer drama, on
the fevers of the great city, the lives and deaths that surged
around him. Instead, he clung to semblances, mindful
against the warning of the apostle, of "the things which are
seen." Flimsy child of a tin-can culture, he so declared
day after day his kinship with us all; the tragic break, like
the breaking of bones or dry sticks; the spirit's empery
endangered, our unsteady throne, the fantastical life of
the senses, squatting in blind sockets like lidless taran-
tulas.

He spoke little, a prelude to the Great Silence, a monastic
rehearsal. Like others, only in a rare moment does a patient
warm up, wax lyrical or prophetical as to his fate. Mostly
silent, mostly abed; those who can walk about do so, some
with purpose, some in a fix of stunned bewilderment.

I close my eyes and imagine the wards as a symphony of
brain waves, the sounds, except for a breakaway groan or
cry, inaudible to the ear of sense. I hear bank upon bank of
music, high C to basso profundo, strings, horns, a massive
beat; vocal, fierce, openmouthed, the dying make a great
din and to-do, their preliminary tuning up for the big open-

ing. Jack comes in, takes his seat somewhere to left front, alto trombone. Long notes, good breath, steady, he raises it sweet and strong; a Latin beat, wrapping the heart around, tight as a shroud, a swaddling band. . .

In those last months, something momentous happened, a gift. He was given faith.

You could almost see that stream, that mystery coming toward him, a rivulet of light among the cups and plates, the bedpans and smells and burnt-out lives; coming toward him down the hall, weaving in and out of the din, the polluting tube. A river of paradise. He bowed forward, tough, unbreakable, and drank. "Fadda, I went to communion this monnin." He announced it in a voice that got progressively fogged, graveled. He had the look by now of a casualty out of *Catch 22*, his nose a sack of cotton and gauze, intermittently bloodied or freshly changed. Into the sack his words fell and died like clots of blood.

They came and went, the living, the ghosts of the living, in the beds around. He stared through them as you would stare down a ghost, he hewed to his own track.

Old hole-in-the-face, all mucus and mess; can I forget that day? He beckoned me, he had a secret. ". . . Went to communion this monnin, everything's ok." Ravaged mouth, eyes ablaze, the hole in his face, as though trigger-happy fate had caught him in its gun sights. . .

Nose: function, to smell out the vagrant or errant or seductive, the hideous, decaying caducous aspects of life.
Nose: most spiritual of the senses, as in "odor of sanctity."
Least attractive in function; as in "to blow the nose."
Humorous: schnozzle, beak, pug.
Contempt: to thumb the nose.
Affectionate: to rub noses.
Curious: to nose about, to nose out, to snoop.

We know what it is to be eyeless or speechless. Some have lost a limb, like a stick falling off a lazy load.

But who of us has lost a nose? Has had the Bad Giant crunch it off like peanut brittle or fish and chips?

We lose one of our body's limbs; the loss is hideously apparent, doubly bizarre in a world where being equipped with everything appetitive and appetizing, noses to roses, is simply to be the compleat American. . .

Tough, tough, Jack was lashed together with whipcord and cat gut, his bones were fused rock. To know why he lasted, you must raise every component of creation to a second power. Tougher than winter or summer scalding, dumped on by buckets from the ramparts, he outwitted, outraced, outlasted it all.

I pictured his soul. It was a cube of adamant, "from which all things came," the magians tell us; indestructible, alight, energetic. . .

The routine of the hospital tends toward the monastic, TV apart.

Jack, a successful entrepreneur of disaster, at length fell back on reflection. He began to hearken to deeper rhythms, those sounds of silence never, if one can credit the Buddhists, entirely quenched, even in rackety souls. Abed or on his feet, he spent more time alone, walked with deliberate tread, turned away from us that public and punch-drunk face. And became, toward the end, a facsimile of a quite presentable monk: prayerful, celibate, and poor.

A long time dying, he died in no time at all, a monk with a mandate. In the TV room, fittingly, among the absurd, spurious flickers of the cultural embers, the death of practically everything, he passed *ex imaginibus et umbris in veritatem*. It was toward three in the afternoon of a summer day. The tube blared, the sales pitch faded. Ironsides the wheelchair cop, rolled on stage. Jack settled back, put a match to a cigarette. Then he arched forward in spasm, his soul spun off like a Catherine wheel of blood. Simply and terrifyingly, he exploded to the floor.

Thus he showed at the last, the combustible impatience of his lifetime; to become at length what the world and himself, his worst enemies, with appallingly successful purpose, had kept him from being. For a whole lifetime. This is why he burst his bonds and went up in blood. Like a gigantic bound captive; like an image of superstate; like most citizens of such a state. To understand his folly, his sanguinary end, his accouterment of splendor, one must come to his life through the maze of forces, booby traps, detours, half-truths, blind alleys set in the human path, wickedly smiling, persuasive, destructive, set against holiness and community and life itself.

Cultural traps, traps of the soul. For the culture is the surrounding radiance of the soul, its outreach, its mirror, as Plato tells us. And the soul is the concentrated energy of the larger light. Together they surpass, grow, possess themselves and the world. Or they fasten on one another, hearken to conquest, violence, lust; become mutually destroying angels, and perish.

Thus our plight. Fictions harass, lord it over, images of truth grow testy, devious, self-clouded. The ego inflates, reaches outward for the commonweal, seizes on it, devours it. The truth of existence? It is no longer precious, there are other goods, louder voices. We lust after the lesser life and despise the greater; and so lose all. . .

So long Jack, old streetwise one, old sweet and sour. Some go easy, some epitaphs are simple, some lives flow to their ending like the river, like the sundown. You hardly knew they were around, the difference they make is slight indeed to us, dimwits who walk in the light of others and never pause to lift hands in wonder.

Not you, not how you went. A deathbed is, after all, not a battlefield. But you died as though by a tossed grenade; your last moments had the bloody, wanton pomp of a street fray; death was a mugger, it clubbed you down. And got away free, and left a sorry burden to the survivors, who in deaths like yours (the death of children, a real bombardment, war's midnight marauders, midday furies, all the deaths we live with and can do nothing about) must clean up the blood and decently bury the victims. And go on, the blank look of those who trudge the long way round a short and simple hope; and so finally accept what we cannot fathom.

After such a death, one lifts empty hands. Insight, mutual comfort, tears, outcome. Where? A limp look, a resigned shrug; we mutter, "Things could be worse."

Then, perhaps, someone objects, pushes matters. "Indeed. How could they be worse?"

You fumble through yesterday and feint toward tomorrow, come out with a try; things could be worse—if there were no faith; no one, I mean, to have faith in.

Then it comes with a rush. No one to receive Jack, no one to welcome him, to pick up the pole-axed, violated being drowning in his own blood. No one to set him on his feet, set him in motion, on another ground. No one, on part of Jack, to be responsible to, to be answered to, no judge. No one to speak for him, no advocate. Nothing. Only this slack, empty, five-feet-ten shell, this quondam human. . .

No one? Our knees turn to water, we are at the brink. There are violations, crimes beyond measure; we are torn apart by the absurd. Words we rejoice in, smoothly savor on the tongue—life, reality, entelechy, coherent world, spirit and its incarnation—all lie at our feet, a mockery, an ungainly doll, a grimace of life.

Someone, another side of death. Write this down. For

this terrible death, this bootless life, I forgive Christ. I forgive him the blood, the whimper, the collapse, the smell, the terror of those about, their gaze of horror (themselves on their last legs, immobilized in their places), the TV ranting on, a demented bedlam.

To forgive is presumptuous, a matter that should not arise?

Perhaps not. And yet, would an unforgivable God, a God beyond offense or accounting, be an improvement on our lot? A God to whom matters of blood and waste, lives that stagger and impede, deaths that signify nothing—to whom such matters could not be credited, debited? "Come down, come down, you great one," we cry out, "no Olympians need apply."

It comes home to me, no Olympian applied, but a dying man.

The thief on his left, that braggard, at a certain point took counsel with himself, as the guilty now and again are led to do, even the worst. He grew thoughtful, he climbed down from his gallows and crossed over, left side to right, and climbed up again.

Then he changed his tune, mockery to entreaty. "Lord remember me."

Thus, there were at the end those two: the rabbi, doomed, discredited. And one thief only, the unlikely saint of the last hour, companion in death, his blood mingling with innocent blood, one stream, one outcome.

The thief had to die. About this, Christ could do nothing; any more than in his own cause, bound over as he was, beyond recourse. The thief had to die; but he did not have to die badly.

He turned to one who turned to him, whose majestic mien was a defiance, an unknown terrain—that mysterious figure of woe, on whom the trap fell, for no discernible

crime (yet lucid, in command, refusing the sop, not cring-
ing at the inevitable, the retributive jaws that held him fast).

We have to die, we do not have to die badly. I leave the
discussion of this to another time. But for the difference
between the two, which I take to be of some moment, to
Jack, to us all, I thank Christ.

For presenting to our eyes so bloody an ikon, so defaced
an image of the divine.

For daring also to die well, though in distress, aban-
doned.

And because he died in this way, deflating the Olym-
pian, exalting the human most strangely, the flare of a lamp
on a night of fury, I also forgive him.

I forgive him the death of Jack, the death of all who die in
like circumstance, in a world which seems at times no more
than a hideous, painted mimesis of crucifixion. A world in
which the vocation of humans (all variety of religions and
skins and cultures laid aside; as in the old paintings of
Christ's death, his outer garments and those of his killers
were laid aside)—that vocation seems atrociously narrowed
to two: torturer and victim.

The Christ who so died can be forgiven, he is subject of
my forgiveness. Since he is responsible beyond doubt for
the narrowing gauge of the world, its murderous intent and
scope, the evil that daily rises to him or falls upon him
(upon his cosmic body, we are told), the evil he can not, or
will not, cancel out.

We hold him accountable, as we hold one another ac-
countable. Indeed, in forgiveness of him, as of one another,
we vindicate the dignity of the offender; we say, "You are
recusant but responsible." Divine or human, it seems to me
the analogy holds, a hand upon a sworn truth.

Forgiveness is also an act of respect; I bow in spirit before
the one I forgive. I say in my heart, "I ignore or despise you

or refuse you at great risk, bound up as I am with you, in humanity, in denial of humanity . . . two prisoners bound and blindfolded, back to back, to work out their fate."

But to forgive God?

It seems to me a question of faith, rightly understood. Not of faithlessness or presumption. The cry of Job, the cry of the victims under the altar, these are not stifled, silenced. These are ikons of faith, ikons that have taken voice, to raise a cry, to declare the horror implicit in a justice forever deferred. They are cries that render God accountable in His world.

I think today of our nuclear impasse, the unthinkable crime that sets about, with a mad iciness, to bring down the heavens, to destroy the earth and all life. What part does God have in such crime, the final crime, reaching to the height and depth of creation itself, the crime against the seven days of creation?

This part. He does not intervene.

He is silent. He plays the game of the ninth hour, of the agony of Jesus, and his death. "Why have you abandoned me?" The question hovers on the air, unanswered, to our own day.

He plays to the utmost the game of the lover of freedom, the one who makes of our freedom, even in its malicious and depraved forms, his showcase, his dark pride and joy. "Let them be free, even to the denial of me, even to their own destruction."

I call him to account for this, I see in such words (imagined or deduced) an affront to self-declared goodness, his solicitous providence. I will cry out. I will be slow to forgive this crime which allows criminals their day, the crime of nonintervention.

I will not easily surrender before a god in the image of the complicit, silent ones, the evaders. Their god is not my

God. Let his conduct in the world match that of the holy
one, the messiah, the lover of the poor and victims. . .
    Forgiveness. One's life proceeds; a slow, dragging pro-
cess leading, as one hopes, to an obscure reconciliation.
Something by no means achieved, an achievement ironi-
cally delayed by grace itself, since the grace that would
accept, reconcile, unify, is the grace that forbids an out-
come too easily or summarily achieved. Not too easily, not
cheaply! Let the contention go on!
    His own symbols give him away, are signs of contention.
    In Revelation (not to speak of other books of Scripture),
he is both the lamb who unseals the meaning of world and
event, and the first horseman who set historic forces in
motion, wildly, irrevocably. Unmasker of illusion, enemy
of secrecy and double-dealing; and on the other hand, iden-
tified with history itself (especially in the breakneck
technological stampede); first of the horsemen, in concert
with plague, violence, famine, ecological and ethical disas-
ter. In their company, releasing them all, allowing them a
measure of bloody autonomy, leading them forth.
    Irresponsibly? Or with strict ethical accountability, fi-
nally to be judged? (I mean himself, too, "finally to be
judged.")
    May one so regard the activity of God in the world?
Applying to him the act of forgiveness, even delaying for-
giveness, making of one's life a troubled progress toward
rapprochement, forbidding ecstasy until justice is achieved,
calling the Divine One (as well as humans, as well as one's
self) to accounts?
    Not much of a life, not much of a religious life.
    And then I reflect on the alternatives.
    For one, a kind of many-faced idolatry. The setting up,
as though by common consent or drift, "Christian" West
and "atheistic" East, in numberless bunkers and banks and

highly placed lives, of "false gods before him." Gods of death, idols of ego, countercultural absurdities, drunken facsimiles of the good life, unsavory connections with pollutive systems, the stocks and stones our hearts bow down before. . .

Rest in peace, old Jack in the box. Your death induces in my soul, all unexpected, a mood of chastened orthodoxy. I move in a constant twilight, enough light for the next step, barely. My mood compounded, ill-mixed, revolt and resignation. Only rarely, a moment of true forgiveness, peaceableness. The crimes of the world, the criminal state of authority, weigh me down. Did Jesus not order things differently, did he not die in order that no one need die, needlessly, absurdly; in order that death be neither blind fate, punishment, curse—but entrance into glory? I bow my neck (though I straighten up again, unrehabilitated) before this pressure of wills, this mystery darkening to enigma.

And I cry out, "You have promised to be with us all days, where are you? And even granted you are in our midst, what difference do you make?

"Or have you reneged on your promise, shaken off the polluted dust, washed hands of it all?

"And if this is so, are you not acting in criminal fashion, contrary to assurances once offered, in psalm and prophecy, in the witness of the saints—assurance of your faithful love?

"I seek even the dregs of your presence, a hint of something more than rampageous necessity. Show me the divine encompassed in a drop of falling rain, a mote of sun, a spasm of conscience among the swords. . .

"Is this not granting you a great deal? A large dose of absence, a mere iota of presence?

"I do not bring it against you that Jesus fell under the blade of necessity, that he cried out in defiance of death. I struggle to believe; that his very cry was a signal of your presence, your unanswering nearness; that cry which at least now and again refuses to seize as cause of despair or blasphemy.

"Given such a world (the powerless divine, the great bloat of wickedness prevailing)—in such a world, faith barely survives.

"My faith is affront, argument, conflict. I do not come before you well heeled, sleek in spirit, persuasive (nor do you come before me, if you come before me, high and mighty). I am seldom at peace with human arrangements. For those I love, things almost never go well. Against the wall of privilege, caste, blindness and willed violence, we do little more than scratch fingers raw. The consequences of resistance are harsh, and bound to grow more so; the results meager indeed. Who listens, who is advocate, who speaks for the victims?"

I seek a rage of soul that burns and burns, without ever burning up. I turn to Job as to a recognition scene, a text to be learned by heart, to be cried by madmen in the streets, a blessing so near a blasphemy, a call like a curse. I pray for less queasiness and control. Or the rage of James, his diatribes against the rich and duplicitous, those who would make of the church a nest of defamation, of thieves and liars.

In memory of Jack. I summon courage and wit to my side, that I be responsible in the world. And in virtue of that charge, that I hold God responsible for the world.

To be faithful in this task, I must pass over, as did Jesus; from lesser life, from death, to a new creation. Must pass over, as did the thief, and Jack, left hand to right.

For the criminal cannot in good faith utter his "*j'accuse*" to

God, and remain where he was. He is guilty, unregenerate; he does not deserve to be taken seriously. He must first come down from his gibbet, and cross over, change his heart.

Then he gains a hearing. As did the thief, and Jack.

May I be granted a hearing. Understanding, at least in measure, how far those two journeyed before death pitched them over—the measureless distance of rebirth from the left hand to the right hand of God.

Chapter 8

"THE BADGE"
A POEM

When I go down down into the rancid inside of the black bull's gut
    West 96th to Chambers
I think of Persephone, the daughter who was promised a brown bag of
    sweets by the king of hell
Too of the sweet singer & his geetar   who refused to hand
    over his love   to death's icy arms
Who almost made it   but for that longing backward look that canceled
    all
Making honorable pacts into instant ripoff
Since after all is said or sung
You & I know only too well who's in charge here   alas   alas
I think of Dante who plunged into the forest   it lurked there like a
    bristly
    wolf's head   red mouth open   a bloody sunset—
Now it's all bets off. Off.
Everything that makes NY New York wiped out
Racism   povertyism   richism   sexism   grabism
    Catholicism   inhumanism
    marxism
Nothing left of everything   that in the common estimate of church &
    state
    & insurance & world trade & booby traps & massage alleys & jewish
    mayors & christian bone-breaking cops
Everything that made life as they say (& seldom mean) "worth living."
Here we (I mean we) come in like walking bags of bones. Most wear their
    roseate badge which says *Members Only. All Others Go Get Lost on the*
    Franklin Roosevelt Drive, Jogging, Running from Pace-setting Death
Those who don't merit a merit badge as yet   come in and make
    points.
    Small   change;   comfort   feed   joke   jostle   These   are
    exactly
17¼ points toward the Jigantic Jackpot

One more point   What you die of is what you live off. I don't
know in the least what this means, it's a sulfurous statement
out of the third chapter of B'more catechism #3, "On hell and
the 3 other last things."
As to the badge. Rule is: wear it anywhere. On some it is checked daily,
shined up, attached a bit to right or left, up or down. The rule is:
wear it to bed   to potty   to whirlpool   to chapel.
You wear it when your skull starts turning like a ferris wheel   bearing
you aloft from light of earth to light of heaven & lightheartedly
back down & then upsy daisy again.
Do I have my badge on? some check it out spasmodically in their
last moments like debutantes at the doorway of glory.
Covered or bare they keep fretting, *Is it there?* They die of it   they get
reborn of it.
It's pinned on you   by the Prize Donor—
Nose   mouth   eye   shoulderblade   lower neck   ab-
    domen   crotch
    thigh   shin   foot. Such variety! Then the hidden one;
    imagine
The petrified recruit; the Big Donor pins
    the medal to the inside of a skull or the outside of the brain's
    grey convolute   fastens it in place in the narrows between tissue
    and bone
The badge is a living thing after all, perceptions of its own as to
    right and wrong, befitting and bizarre.
Shortly after the ceremony,
    it begins to raise very hell! Like an ant colony stuck in concrete, like
    a buried sand fly
Like the irrepressible passion of a prisoner, he's unkillable! a Houdini
    of the spirit condemned to hell by secular gods
Patience! He conquers the masked brutalities of that place
    he bellows and batters his way OUT
Viola, this badge, this emblem gets heard from, made visible—
It cracks the pate, it makes little feathery purple veins in the skin of
    the skull, like the veins on an alcoholic schnozzle
(Only these lie directly on the bone, scarcely concealed by a filament of
    skin, they cling there, crawl there like ivy on stone, in winter
    when the leaves are gone.)
Or it makes an epiphany in the gut like an inadvertent oyster anxious to
    please and lo!

Discomfort mounts, the belly puffs up in contrariety to nature
Now you are 17 months pregnant
The system backlogs
Finally and in any case, a bang! as of a hatched bullet
It's good night sweet gander   Your goose is cooked.
Or to keep our original image
Your badge is your best bet
You're now—
Come in!
—in good standing
for
the
duration.

Chapter 9

THREE WHO WENT EASY

Big Eyes

One or another look like a doll's head cut from its sacking and straw body, then, by some mishap, melted down, a plastic left too near the heat. . . .

The solids blister, run, bubble, leaving the face a hideous glomerate—just enough of a face to make you shudder, so much is missing. A face, you say to yourself, is meant to hear and talk and see. But such faces! One sense working overtime, adapting, doing the work of the others.

"So you're the priest, etc., etc.," said to me the wife of one such Singular Sense. "My husband and I are of course awahe of you and your brothuh." (But her spouse could verify only by two nailed eyes that he was aware of anything.) She rattled on, she was grandiose, by turns a gloomy Cassandra, a diva. "Yahs, he came from the VA hospital, had radical vertical horizontal coaxial chemotherapeutic et cetera; after which as yew may see as well as ah, he's just about good as new, awl things considered; and certinly gentle as a spring lamb in grahs, don't you think, Fathah? . . . And next week being Thanksgivin, won't we all have a merry to-do for ahselves, one and all, plenty of turkey and fixins as the sisters guarantee, so sublahm of them to include not only my husband. . . ." (A sweeping gesture like a snickersnee on a thong, toward the poor shankbone on the bed.)

And I thought, Oh Jesus, what a feast it'll be when we wheel in this poor pièce de résistance for the knife and fork of the Appetitive One; and what a grandiose jaw will fall when Hungry McAmerica falls to on Mother Hubbard's gaunt offering!

He lies there dumb as his effigy; you have no idea (maybe you have) how many characters the eyes can mime, how quickly the eyes learn the lines, skillful stand-ins for ears and mouth and nostrils. He not only sees with his eyes, a fairly standard skill—with his eyes he talks and listens and smells and kisses and consigns you to center stage or outer darkness. Most of all and best of all, his eyes simply listen.

And this is a skill, I thought with a pang, proper to paradise, not to our spoiled acres; proper to practically all beings who queasily spend their lives surviving against odds, playing Patience or Charades, while the rest of us bounce about like shuttlecocks or buckshot out of a blind barrel, banging off walls, bringing down, bang, bang, wooden-headed ducks like ourselves.

No, creation dumbfounds; it stands stock still and listens. Pick up a stone or a shell, they're just listening. Attentive, cocked, indrawn, sufficient unto.

Why do you think the rain makes the sound it does? I don't mean when it strikes roofs or terra firma or macadam; but in midair, the rain that practically floats there, pauses there, listening. The sound before the sounds.

Off Block Island, a wave gathers strength like a seated woman of marble slowly standing. A sound of garments subtly displaced, she's a goddess of unspent thunders.

And the sunlight on a blinding day in open country, the breezes hold their breath, time stops in its tracks; there's a quality in the air, waiting behind our eyes, as though the soul of things were asking: "What will they see, if ever they see?"

Big Eyes there on the bed, whose orbs are nearly all the mortal equipment left to him, he isn't so much seeing as listening, attending, being. It's the closest thing, the nearest gift, to what Buddhists and Christians call "the Way," the life underlying life.

Poor part of me, the surgeons hacked and carved you like an injected animal, some mad feast of the mind. They left you with too little and too much—too much for my bearing. They cut away the thick casing, they cut the fat and husk away, they peeled layer on layer of expendable flesh and bone. . . . What a dangerous game they played, that coven of inventive dwarfs; Let's show the world what a soul looks like, uncapped from its skull! Let's edge as close to the invisible as the visible may dare. . . . The instruments went chip chop, from crude to cunning; they used and threw aside the mallets and choppers and big blades. And finally they were peeling away, not skin but film, not film but mist, the last layer of pentimento (the frowning mouth of the *Mona Lisa* that concealed the truth, the inscrutable buried smile; the gold leaf on the halo of the saint that overlay the dark scowl of original Cain). . . .

You hover above the bed, poor soul, spirit barely imprisoned, bird of paradise. Will you puff and disappear in thin air? Will the invisible thread that anchors you snap one day, once and for all? Good-bye, away, away.

The Lucky Heir

This one's a skinny little guy; he shakes the scales down no more than a sack of feathers.

Jaunty, Chaplin, Chevalier (humor coming hard in such a place, and dancing never).

I like him. He doesn't know what's up, or he pretends he doesn't know, pretends so blithely it comes to the same thing. Picture him in a straw skimmer, striped pants, a terror amid the ladies, turn of century, June, Atlantic City boardwalk.

"Medicine'll be around at four, think you can hold out?" sister asks jauntily, an elbow in the ribs, spiritually speaking.

"Only if I can have you long with it," he comes back, a demon leer.

She blushes and pushes her dope car away for the next fix.

He's hooked on a chocolate drink, a bowl of vanilla cookies. No great claim on the world, you could hustle pretty much the same items in any shack of the benighted world.

He's taking out of the planet only about ten times the weight he brought into it. That's not an unfair arrangement; especially when you think of the huge agglomeration of fat and funk most of us plan to cheat the frontier guards with. We sweat in shame, the shame of terminal cupidity. Like a shah, like a Farouk, madly lugging it all across. Or failing that (we're always failing that), conniving to leave our baggage, our ill-gottens, in the concupiscent hands of others, stronger, more grasping than our own ("to you with failing hands. . .").

In consequence of which, our legally certified like-minded heirs proceed to dust off the illusions of possession that keep them running with the running dogs.

Thus the last will and testament of one Christian becomes the first and only testament of the next—a testament in each case infinitely more influential, more binding, more fang-toothed than that other one; that other lost in some Aladdin's cave, buried out of sight and mind in an earthen jar; the document that, it was once believed, took a dim view of generational hit and run.

Well. The moral of all this lights up the frail bones of old Norbert; he twitches in his sleep like a dog on a fresh spoor; he's ignorant as a firefly of his own trail of light.

The moral is older than you or I or him or G. Washington or the Banco S. Spirito or medieval merlins or the cave artists of Lescaux. Something, in fact, about a couple in a grove, out of countenance, turned away from one another, a summer of discontent. A horrible taste lies on their tongue; each bears the look of one who, after swallowing, finds half a worm backing out of the fruit.

The lesson of their fall from grace they learned too late to be of help to themselves, or perhaps to us, their legatees; namely:

The apple you eat you can't keep.

Or

Take the bite, the bite's on you.

The Man Who Built the City

Sister took me down to the workshop. She said, "You'll have to see our doll's house builder."

And there he was, and there it was, man and house, he studious and big-boned and ugly—formerly I was told, a builder of real row houses in Queens.

And come to this, as though the angel of a four-cornered universe were cutting him and his houses down to size. To show perhaps for a joke (but a serious one) the Tom Thumb character of Ilium or New York's topless towers, the true size of the soul that animates us.

He was working on a two-by-five-by-five-foot row house of red brick and yellow stucco, a doll's house out of Williamsburg or Baltimore, everything but the front stoop in place. Sister said, "Come, look inside." Sure enough, I peered into a front hallway: a staircase, railings and steps cunningly fitted. She reached in; it was like that old-fashioned game we used to call "fish pond," a carnival where you paid your dime and threw in a line and pulled out a prize in a paper bag. There in her hand she held a four-inch refrigerator with a door that opened (I opened it), and a freezer. Then she fished again, out came a kitchen range, oven and all.

He sat there without a word, bent over his work. That face of his! It was growing. I don't know how else to say it, the face of a sixty-year-old man was growing like a honeycomb, one of the wild kind glued to a tree branch, now and again suggesting the look of a human profile. Or like the chanciness in mountain profiles or clouds; we look, a stab of recognition strikes us. We point and say, "Look, a man's face."

This face was literally growing, changing, like a cloud, but of the earth, weighty. As though barnacles were building a face, or coral. Here, it was cancer-the-builder. His face was building under the hands of death, skin and flesh chancily pasted on here, plucked off there.

In other patients, death is hidden in guts, a leaven, or flares out on the tympanum like a pointed skullcap. Here in a mad twist of humor it built a face upon a face; a millimeter here, an imbalance there, a second tip on the nose, a node on the lip clinging like a drunken bee to a flower.

He went on with his work, his shaky hands fitting a tiny window frame to its wall. Sister and I could ooh and aah and open his oven door and squint down his stairway for all he cared. He went on stolidly, his hulk bent over the wood and paint, calculating the inches, the fractions that joined and separated, everything neat, dovetailed, sanded fine.

And I thought, he wants to leave in the world an exact diminished replica of his life, its human handiwork reduced with finesse and exactitude to the measure of a child's space, a child's extravagant (but after all modest) desire.

He was not repudiating his life, the doll's house was no grimace over his shoulder, no mockery. He was simply assembling his past, in the only way open to his failing strength, his unfailing skills, timbers, and flooring; hoisting it all up, setting it in place. Casting it too, against the weight and strength of the powers bearing down on him; grace against gravity, life battling the closing door.

The doll's house was all that; the core of human endeavor, exquisite, irreducible; trials and errors, good calculation and bad, losses and gains; the house that would stand when he was gone.

The house that stood for him. An anonymous house, street unknown, the great street of the city, of "gold clear as translucent glass." A city "whose wall is jasper" and the city (the seer must repeat it, the glory is beyond imagining) "all of gold clear as glass." Every house for Everyman, a house in high heaven.

As we left the workroom, he was laying a charcoal pencil to an inner wall of the dwelling. A stair would go there; not a beautiful conception, Pierrot's floating dream. It was more like an apprentice blueprint, anchored and solid and true. It was his own, the true angle of his mind, his upward trudge, the workman's ascent to God. And some child would glory in the gift.

What will it mean, child, to dwell in the house of a builder whose last days were passed in raising a roof for your delight? Will his ghost dwell there, diminished?

By no means diminished. Under this roof, less will be more. My father's mansion. Come in.

Chapter 10

THE MIRACLE OF THE
WEEPING BRONZE

There was a cop in our midst; he used to weave up and down the hallways. Things were bad for him, a worm in his brain, a horror invisible to the eye.

The most literal people in the world are also, strangely, great makers of myth. The myth goes like this: A good cop doesn't go wormy. And if the unthinkable happens, and the worm that dieth not gains entrance, why then all should be decently hidden away from the public stare. Which in fact it was, almost until the end.

At first he played mum, not a word. Nor did he so much as volunteer his name. When I introduced myself, his hand shot out, it might have been a stick of wood for all the heart in it. A notable lack of enthusiasm, I think, is the phrase.

Very much cop. Alone, he'd hitch up his pajamas there in the hall, a solitudinous gesture if ever I saw one; high noon, a practice hitch, the burden of the custodian of conscience, the watchman, pacer of ramparts. Lonely; the aura lay on his eyes like a smudge, the loneliness of one who, out of the blue, finds himself stuck in a blind alley, the knife at his neck, the fists working him over. . .

He'd stand there alone, hitch up, as though it made a difference, as though the eyes casing him there in the shadows could be turned irresolute, turned back by so pitiful a show of force. As though death, like a street tough, could be halted by a gesture—pull back, strike a bargain.

He'd hitch up, as though the flimsy pajama pockets still held all the bulging equipment, the gun, the big pad and pen, the walkie-talkie, stick, ID, all the show and panoply of copdom. Alas, the pants sagged at half-mast, the flag was limp, there was death in the precinct.

He knew who I was. It's a look you can't miss among the Catholics; they know who you are, spots break out on you, spontaneously, like measles, under that Look. Barely Acceptable; that's my baptismal name.

The Irish put on their uniforms: clerics, cops, soldiers; then I appear and things get worse. The inner monologue starts, right out of Joyce: What's this type doing here, ragged clothes, sacramental slump? And things normally go from not good to not better.

But not always. Cancer, to coin a phrase, is a great healer. It works patiently, changes come slowly, you can't hasten things. It sits back, wary and wide of eye, a coiled snake on the belly of a sleeper. . .

I decided to imitate the healer.

The cop lasted a long time, months. And so did I. I kept the greetings coming, the small talk you deliver with all the heart you can muster. You talk about the weather, they take your word for it, staring out, listless or resigned or envious from their glass prison, like fish in a tank watching the humans. You inquire about food, appetite, families; keep the lines open. You don't have much of a world to report on, but arguably better than theirs, that room of Poe's with the silently closing walls, that box of night.

The cop began to defrost. Started to unbuckle his equipment, so to speak. He was like a cop coming home from a tough beat to a bridal bed. Off with the holster, gun, walkie-talkie, summons pad, the hat, the big black jacket.

He was gaining that bridal look, too, closing the door on it all, the vitriol, the original sin, the blood and guts, the stiff upper. Something of pathos creeping up on him, taking over, his look at long last daring to meet mine, the look of

the lucky dying. I thought of the Hopkins poem: "Sickness
broke him; impatient he cursed at first. . ."

The clan would gather, upright, uptight. More cops than
you could shake a nightstick at: brothers, cousins. (In New
York cops, like crooks, go in pairs. Among the New York
Irish, cops even run in families, like Catholicism, a per-
petual evidence, unassailable, of the truth of original sin—
transmitted indeed, but transcended as well.)

The look they leveled at me could by no stretch of liter-
ary elasticity be called favorable. Therefore, I will not call it
that. Say, rather, it resembled the apocalyptic glint of a
leveled gun. Not that I was to be accounted necessarily a
danger in the streets. Something more terrible by far: Was I
not wreaking havoc in the heavens, blundering about in the
sanctuary, overturning the holy furniture, the symbols? A
priest breaking the law? What next, their eyes blazed, what
in God's name next?

Cancer in the brain, priests in the Pentagon, sure as hell
it was a crazy world. One intricate crazy web, no begin-
ning, no end. Nothing in the catechism prepared for it,
nothing in the Vatican Council. The family, the dying cop
sat there, high and dry. Urban American gothic, stunned
bewilderment. Where did you go when nothing made sense
any more, a good man dying before his time, weaving about
unsteady as a street wino, in a cancer hospital haunted by a
law-breaking cleric?

They were like seven brothers in an old folktale, which I
hereby invent. In a blind cave after the deluge, seven sur-
vivors built a mockup of the world. All seven of them to-
gether, out of boredom and frenzy, to get things started
again, built a world in a cave. Then they lay down to sleep.
And in the morning the world had grown four legs and
galloped away. Out of the cave, out of sight, out of control.

Now what to do? If the brothers leave the cave, the world

(their world once) may do—what? Turn on them? Eat them alive? Trample them under? Shout, scream, talk conundrums, explode?

And if they stay in the cave, then what? Who wants to eat mushrooms all his life, live blind, die in the dark. . . ?

The months went by, the family stood by; holy mother church, the cave, the solid present; not so solid admittedly as once, but still. . . . They came and went, we traded hellos and goodbyes, polite and distant. They came in on cats' feet, uneasy and inarticulate; left with that half-acknowledged half-stifled sigh of relief with which one turns away from a wake or a graveside. For them, life still was open. There were families, parishes, jobs, outings; I heard talk of a wedding; life intruded.

And all the while, Cop Tim was undergoing his sea changes. Now, at length, he looked at me straight; it was the look the drowning send shoreward: Goodbye. His head was like a faulty gyroscope—he listed to left, to right, dragged an arm and a leg, was semicoherent in speech.

And with Tim and me his evident dying was never the issue at all; it was no more than a speck in the eye of the beholder. . .

Dear reader, you must journey far, beyond appearances and velleities and fictions. You must leave your low-vaulted past, as the poet advised, your precious skin, your many-voiced certainties. And at length you will come to a stillness, a center.

If you wish to befriend the dying, if you become their figure of permanence, their landmark, if the dying long to see you, take jealous note of your absence or inattention—it can only be because, at length, after much travail, your eye takes on the absolute stillness of a serpent on the breast of a sleeper. Or better, the stillness of that sleeper.

Takes on that look which many of the dying, shortly

before the end, achieve. The look which in midair has met the look of the dying. The look that, on both sides, pierces deeper than words can, than health can, than ego, than conjuring or incanting daily existence with its baited fly trap of normalcy; deeper than death itself, crossing the eyes like a cloud across the sun. The look that puts death to rout.

We began to get somewhere, the cop and I. I would hold a light to his cigarette, he was all atremble and shamed, and a current would pass between us. The armaments fell away, the uniform, the past, death the stripper, the old law and the new, the newer law and the newest (always the law, always and everywhere, but not now). We were like two skeletons, chalky hand in hand, on a search that was half-dance, the dance of death, the search for that Lost Kingdom of Spare Parts, the Thrift Shop in the Sky, the Kingdom of Feisty Bones.

His wife helped. I used to watch that cool lady come in, a river of cool, aid freely offered. She'd greet the other lingerers on the ward, as though our doomed clan were as normal as the nightly clot of omadhauns in a neighborhood bar. A most likely cop's spouse, in from Queens, row house, strapping kids, the loyal nightrider, and vigilant. Unlikely too; her face held much peace, or better, peacemaking; head high among the drooping specimens, hair cropped, very much on the qui vive; a little too bright of eye I said to my numen, normalcy a bit forced (but whose wouldn't be?). By no means struck dumb by her fate or his, capable of a willful, upbeat ceremony.

She hauled the kids in with her day after day. Whatever cajoling or fighting preceded, it all stopped on Jackson Street. The sprats came in, raw, noncommittal, shortly grew bored, yawned, after five minutes were squatting like frogs, fixated on the TV.

Then one day, as they say in the precinct, came my

break. It was pure luck, none of my making, that falling together of pieces. Something a cop waits for, or a writer, a true believer, something akin to grace; a bolt in the blue.

I was going around the wards toward the end of the day, saying my weekly goodbyes. In the hospital, it should be explained, goodbyes are not taken or given lightly. You say goodbye, you come back a week later, you may find the friend you said your farewell to; or then again you may not, you search in vain. The hospital in this instance, as in many others, a place where one had best mean what one says, the easy garrulities of street and school and pulpit having no place here. Shockingly, goodbye means what it says: a phrase to start a journey, God go with you. To three at least or four or (around Christmas or Easter when for some reason more than usual get started on their journey) to as many as six or seven, you won't be saying anything more, not a week later or a year or a lifetime.

I came in, stood at Tim's bed. Wife in attendance, as usual, today, as every day since he was struck down.

Today, the shocker.

Even as he faded week by week, he and she made common front against the onslaught. To outsiders like myself, their bad times were matters of guesswork. To the world, the motto on the escutcheon went something like *ars gratia artis;* or maybe *blood is thicker than brawn.* In any case, they dredged up their battered smiles out of some deep mine, a common pact or wedding vow. I marveled: the pudor of the marriage bed around the deathbed.

Not that day. And because not that day, never again. Things never again the same. The routine, the routine of dying, cracked like a living egg. There lay my prideful cop, my paragon and paradigm, he of the shoulders, the eyes of ice, bone built on bone like the blocks of a precinct in the great city, the living monument, rectitude, religion; that town crier, that stiff "Halt!" in the fact of whatever flotsam the streets flung up—all the rambunctious, insolvent, shifty, unlawful, unlovely. . . . But why go on? He was her heart's desire, he had come to—this.

The unthinkable came to pass. He lay there weeping. I almost add a phrase which would make of the weeping a gentle and poignant and pearly linkage between himself and his childhood. The phrase would be a lie. He was weeping unlike any child in the history of this vale of tears. Weeping like a parched well, like an animal under mallet blows. Tears of shame, loss, humiliation, tears of a proud cop brought low by Mugger Death.

And she, leaning over, remonstrating with him, tender and stern at once, holding a line; but a living line, the line of a bough that bends under weight, a weight of love.

She was like the queen in a play of Ionesco's. She had married in good times, she would not shrink from the bad times. She made love to him in the good times, she would not play whore to his mind in the bad times. She was no sycophant, no base comforter, mistress of illusion. Her upright stance, her suffused eyes, these were her honor, and his.

Now she encompassed him in a ring of adamant—the truth.

Calmly insisting, objecting, correcting, calm drawn from a reservoir of selfhood.

"No, it's not true," again and again; "Not true, no." (She put a finger on his lips.) "They told us from the beginning, they told where this would end, they did everything they could."

And he weeping, shouting his grievances, his betrayal by doctors, by family, by her. That he was never told he was dying, that more could have been done to save him. Wild, remorseless, uncontrolled—his grief.

It was terrible and cleansing. I stood there. It was like watching a monument come to life. Not all at once, since it is not of the quality of stone, even under a miraculous hand, to spring to life all together, in every part, on the instant. Not at once the free flowing of a simulated human form. No, the stone comes to life, cracking, laborious, limb by limb, shaking off its frost and borrowed heat, leaving around a fall of jagged shards.

And last of all, perhaps, the statue would weep.

And that moment we would rightly term miraculous. We would at such a moment consent to believe a miracle has transpired.

I stood there appalled, flooded with joy. I was witnessing a great violation in nature; in the nature of stone, say, or of bronze. Such a transformation, transfiguration, as would imply not only that dead matter lived, but that the bronze or stone had renounced the form in which it had been cast, renounced the limit imposed by its maker. This was the second miracle, or perhaps only the second aspect of the first miracle.

I mean something like this. At an East Side entrance to Central Park stands a hideously typical war memorial, born of the inflated dreams of unconditional winners. On a pedestal, six or seven armed brutes, big as humanoids, are shouting into the wind, bayonets thrust forward, uniforms disheveled. The enemy being, if one follows their deranged looks, all innocent passersby, all the canyon dwellers of Fifth Avenue; with perhaps (I forget) a sideswipe of blades in the direction of the feckless deer and seals of the Park Zoo.

It occurs to me, groping as I do to understand the Miracle of the Weeping Bronze, that the amok soldiers of Eighty-sixth Street, under the ministration of some wonder worker, would not merely come to life, a highly disputable blessing on that svelte neighborhood, but would come to life entirely and spiritually altered as to guise, intent, task. That is to say, casting down their bronze weapons with a clatter, falling to knee, invoking the God of peace and amity, renouncing war and warmaking, chanting like a very explosion of the silent and unconverted years, the Beatitudes of Matthew's Gospel.

Let us also grant them, these transmogrified and reborn ones, the gift of tears.

And with this, we have, in the remorseful and tender overflow of healed nature, our miracle intact.

A week or two after the above scene, my friend died.

To me, his death was redundant. The day the bronze wept, he had joined the living, he belonged to us.

His tears were a borrowed stream, borrowed from upstream, the tears of Christ. They flowed and refreshed us, downstream so to speak, a Jordan, a Ganges; here and now they cleansed the stigma from our brow. And someday, ample, compassionate of breast, the stream that flows and is still, will receive our ashes.

The funeral ritual of Officer Tim was, as all such occasions are, in the hands of others than the one chiefly concerned. In the hands of those, one presumes, who had not yet learned to weep. They covered him, his bark and bones and dry eye sockets, with the flag that purportedly covers all, conceals all, life, crime, sin, betrayal, cops and soldiers and chaplains. The flag, a kind of primitive Reformation symbol, now secularized; which is to say, dipped in human blood; the coping and questionable mercy not of Christ, but of Caesar, a juridical concession symbol; not a forgiveness, a fiction rather than a new start. Or so it was said Luther had taught.

She was proud and tearful; the children, as far as could

be learned, said nothing. And neither did I. But when she showed me photos of the ceremony, I could only think, be comforted my soul. He has escaped it all, surpassed it. And looking on the images of this hydra-headed banquet, this sop tossed to Christ and Mars, I could only say, "Thank God his face was turned aside."

Chapter 11

MURPH THE SURF AND THE OUTGOING TIDE

Murph the Surf is on his last legs. The thought of things to come, not to speak of things present and past, is pestiferously whelming. Murph twitches like a doll on a string, tweaked by the hand of a willful child.

Murph has his reasons. You'd twitch too if you had one tube up your nose and another up your rear, if your frame were broken out in sores, if a hot poker lay on your palate, another up and down your leg like a decoration "pro-life," melting and dripping in the heat of death. Oh, yes, Murph has his reasons.

Anyway, he lies there and I stand there. I stand there holding Murph's left hand. He knows it, in and out. Mostly he's out of it, out of wit, out of action. But then again, most of his life's been a curmudgeonly exit from what the rest of the world said was a stage—in favor of off-stage realities like the next buck and the next bed and everything crepuscular in between.

Murph, so to speak, had a different action in mind. He held things to a standoff, early in life, by a not altogether sporting ploy: a grip on a broken bottle waved with felonious purpose in front of that virginal phiz. Life backed off. Murph was temporarily, oh so temporarily, the winner in a game we used to call Territory.

Alas, there were further rounds. And in their course, the enemy prevailed. Until today; there's hardly enough turf for Murph to stand on. Which he isn't.

When Murph came to our door (as was commonly sup-
posed, to die), story has it he arrived accompanied by the
entire clan Murphy. They were ready to go out together; a
sentiment which in the Murphian sense translated: We're
set for a show of clan devotion, simpatico, with this solitary
voyager. By getting stoned to the eyeballs; together. Thus
did they arrive, simmeringly bellicose, weaving; but on the
positive side, well armed and houseled against the crudities
of the Great Braggard.

Indeed. The Murph's came as they would go, together.
A bonded clan, boasting only a tenuous stake in this world,
the Murph's being, in the exalted sense, street people, free
spirits, grandly contemptuous of the mores of grand
houses, householders, doorways, doormen, and all such as-
sorted binders and loosers. "Bad cess," they cried, to the
mourners, the weepers, the long faces, the mumblers and
mooners, all who court death for a rank living. No, a thou-
sand times no. The Murphys, drunk as lords, were of single
mind in this matter of dying. It must be done according to
hoyle, an ancient liturgy, tears and long libations.

The sister took them in, the quick and the dying. She
settled Murph in a corner bed, decked out in clean and
decent linen. There Murph, composed in soul and body,
would await the Final Pardoner, the one who in his own
sweet time would presumably knock once, enter, and, with
a wave of his palm, set all things to rights for Murph,
forever. More necromancer he would be than pill pusher,
more overland guide than comforter. Far more stern as to
the eyes and brusque as to the tongue than is the common
practice of marveling medicos, those who pad noiselessly
about sickrooms, to assure the dying that they are so far
from dying as the devil is from pardon. Well. An ancient
adage has it: The truth will out, given an escape hatch.

To revert, Clan Murphy is at the door. Sister opens the

door. Dumbfounded. But not for long. She takes counsel in herself; what have we here? Here we have, beyond doubt, four drunk Irishmen of whom one, by the look of his wasted bones and blotched face, is dying. Therefore, I shall do one or two things, which for the sisters of the dying are strictly old hat, even though for most they may lie in the category of the startling. No matter. I will lead this dying specimen Murph to his corner bed, a bed which an Irish king might not scorn to stretch his frame in. As for the other inebriated relative beings, we will leave them to their own devices. They do not for the moment concern us. And she took off, to expedite things. And returned some half-hour later to check the progress of the patient, found Murph neatly composed between sheets, hands folded seemly on breast, whiskered nose turned heavenward, a dress rehearsal of beatitude. Dead (if the expression may be pardoned) to the world.

As to the brethren, by no means departed. Likewise were they composed on various beds, in varying states and angularities and violations, awry with regard to compass north and south, true east and west. This way and that, head this way in one bed, feet that way in another. Collars open, shoes off or on, a pride of noble sleepers, strangely suffused and untidy, the stilled revelry of life affirmed.

Now sister was no fool. One does not play poker against the dying, if one is not to challenge the living as well. Time was when sister won a game here and there; which is to say, she knew well the virtue of losing. What she did on this occasion was to tiptoe about the ward, dealing her cards, making certain all players were muttering healthily in slumber—and tiptoe out again. Such an exit became her, her sublime, maddening, preposterous vocation.

Time passed. The Murphs were long vanished—to occupations, to idleness, to the great world, its convulsions and still points, its drama and the recounting of its drama being much the substance and nub of their Irish souls.

All vanished, save one. Some months have passed since the Murphs, in corporate show of strength and spirit, strode recklessly and with set purpose into our midst. A cruel day is at hand, a nearly final one, as we shall see.

For today Murph is dying in earnest, the decks cleared, the far shore sighted. If he shows a certain explosive reluctance against the final push, if he holds to the sides of the bed as though digging in his heels against the tides that would bear him home, why, who can fault him? Surely not we who watch from our safe country.

I held Murph by the hand. He would soon be dead. I was not comforted by any thought that occurred. So would I die. So would we all. So death was common, vulgar, nefarious, encompassing, would make of us all his brutalized yoke beasts. So so so. Meantime, here lay this puny wasted West Side New York street specimen who, for some thirty-five adult ardently potionary years, regarded church and state and all the cracks in life's boardwalk through the amber prism of a half-empty pint of cheap Burning Bushwack's. And found it good. And swigged away like exposed plumbing; and found it good. And of a sabbath folded to knee as though at a sanctus signal at old St. Paul's Sunday proceedings, and found it good good.

Three socks at the bell and Murph was ushered uptown to St. Luke's, there to be shaken out as to the pockets and hung up to dry like a drunken shroud. And found it good. Well, somewhat. And recovered, only to smoke his lungs leathery as a herring's. And got away with it, except that the cancer surfaced here and there, a hawking, smelly spit at midnight or dawn, what the hell, no big thing.

No? It was a leech, it got big and bigger and eventually bloody. And so back to St. Luke's and the knife.

They opened him up. The masked faces of the surgeons met, like a comical climax in "M*A*S*H"; that look that says it all slightly before God runs in to stake a claim. Sewed him up again. So long Murph, old sack, old sour mash.

That's where we came in, the sisters more precisely, and myself, on the day of Murph's dying. He might last a few hours, even a few days; but for all practical purposes, this is it. Twitch like a calf under an electric prod, mime, curse, flay, flee. Forget it. Boy, you're down to the last redoubt, that four-by-six-foot bed is all the length and width of the earth you'll ever claim again. There's an angel overhead, there's a goose walking over your grave.

Sister came in briskly, padded in like a sanctified cat, brisk and balmy. She held a secret in her neat hand, a glass of darksome inviting amber. Waved it about like a flambeau; it released on the air its heavenly, unsuspected humors. Held it under my nose. "Voilà" she said in a tone of good-humored exasperation. "One last try. If this doesn't work, God knows what will."

Murph had indeed conveyed his contrary frame around its last curve. Nothing, literally nothing in the apothecary way availed to relieve Murph of the pangs of the last hour. Sedatives sent him romping up the wall like a cockroach. Injections that would propel other patients into Sunday a week, rendered Murph bug-eyed night and day.

Sister uncapped his plastic stomach tube. She let it all go down, that Jordan stream, poured into nose and nasal passage and throat and chest and gut the living rope of 120-proof immortality. Purring faintly, down it went, like Wordsworth's virginal brook, down and down, an artless current mightily modifying the climate of this tumultuous soul. The Murphy limbs soared outward on an absolute pacific sea. Murph and the surf were one. . .

Nothing in life became him like the passing from it. Every four hours, that last day, the mighty jolt unraveled his poor, crossed wires, gathered his final fuss into quietness. The whiskey was like a whole Con Ed crew descending into Murph's internal combustion system. Suddenly, everything went right, Murph turned on, turned off, he was fail-safe.

That afternoon I went looking for what was left of him, down the elevator to the hospital morgue. I opened the refrigerator door. Murph would thrash no more, twitch no more. Not all the Panther Juice in the universe would warm his fires again.

I reached in, put my hand to the top of his head. Cold, cold, a life unclaimed, a death that turned things around. For if the life was rack and ruin, a Bowery tale, all stench and failure, at least the death went beyond, transfigured briefly the poor wretch and his lost years.

His gift to the universe and its sightless ironic guardian spirits was modest, better than cough or gasp or curse. It was a racketing from his bowels, it hit his chest like a gong; it bounced off the iron walls of the death house, vanished like the odors from a pulled cork, a Bronx cheer, a surprise, a vulgar rightness. Was it faretheewell, was it here I come? In any case, here's to Murph's last laugh.

ON GETTING NOWHERE, STANDING BY
Notes on Being "Marginal,"
Not Conformed to this World

Margin; a space along the edge where the text is absent. Or a space created by the text itself. Unfancifully, a space where life is blank, unlived, awaited, unarrived.

Marginal; in a contemptuous sense, not part of the text, not part of the scene, irrelevant to the "action." In this sense, the text of life or love or religion is written by and for the winners.

"Marginal" therefore; to have no history.

Please note the irony here. The text of Scripture is commonly thought of as written about the winners (cf. above). But the text is, in fact, written about the losers. More: It is written *by* a loser, also named "friend," "advocate," "messiah."

This may all be true. But then something else, something shocking, an astonishing larceny occurs.

The text is rather quickly snatched, "appropriated" in the scholarly jargon, by the winners. It is thereby violently uprooted from its proper hands, sources, geography, setting. It belonged in hut, knapsack, beggar's hand. It was written to illuminate not merely what happens in the world, but the meaning of that world, its events, eons, cataclysms, pretensions, ironies, futilities; and all this from a special point of view, of the no-account, the losers, the remnant, the "face-to-face community."

Now the text is in other hands. It is captive, colonized, bowdlerized. It has been taken from the edge, the margin of life where it was written, about which scene and folk it was written—to the dead center. Now it is another inert form of property, a dead letter, a hieroglyph.

The text must be stolen back—for the sake of the poor, in all justice. For it belongs to them, their inheritance, their due, their code.

St. Rose's Home is a proper, perhaps a unique, example of the marginal gospel (a tautology if ever there was one) embodied in a place and community. The hospital has no stake in secular largesse. And only such part in the structure of church as may enable the community to borrow and integrate gospel symbols with life and death, here and now. (In such situations of life and death, indeed, the symbols belong, show forth their beauty and energy, flourish.)

The sisters who conduct affairs and orchestrate the drama are themselves marginal. This by reason of their intense adherence to the letter of Christ's promise: "I come quickly." They prepare with all dignity and care for his return; an event which occurs daily here, in the death of the old and young and abandoned and affluent (rarely) and alcoholic and degraded and dazed and fear-ridden—all brought to the same level of helplessness and waiting, all accorded a like love. This is a rare place where true benefits are cheerfully given. A sign might be hung out: *Come and go freely; your money is no good here.*

The dying are, of course, marginal to the living, to "normal" life as commonly understood. But death (and life as well) are stripped, in such a place as this, of their clinging horror. From being cast out by the living, the dying are taken up, cherished. In the hospital, moreover, a secular promise is unmasked of its spurious pretense. The promise is constantly proclaimed and just as promptly and brutally violated; it has in fact become the nemesis of the poor, we see its cynical force in the condition of our patients. They arrive at the hospital, having been anesthetized, grotesquely mutilated, experimented on, bombarded with radiation, chemically altered in the brain, deceived as to their true condition and chance for survival.

And finally they are cast out of hospitals and nursing homes, many of which dread their deaths as yet another bad mark in the account books.

The secular promise goes somewhat this way: Through techniques of medicine, one attains immortality. Or again: You need not die, you may live on indefinitely.

All such nonsense is finished for our patients. They arrive at our door dislocated, frantic, people without a country. Cast out, transferred, their time on earth appreciably shortened by yet another shock, setback, rejection.

Nonetheless, most of them cheer up under the canopy of loving concern outspread over them. Most, in consequence, make a good death.

Why do I go to the hospital? Something like this. To find a way of verifying an animal intuition; understanding as I do that the only way I can live today, short of living off others, being complicit in their suffering and poverty, is in a marginal situation.

Or again, to undo the secular dread of death, and replace

it with the exhilaration of a promise which is death's true denial and undoing.

To let go so I could let come.

Also, to alter the expectation of the dying as to the function of a priest. I appear at bedside to greet them, hold their hands. I am dressed in old clothes, ready for whatever service seems required or helpful. They can take me or leave, as can the nuns, orderlies, families. I do not bring the holy oils, or pray the sacrament of the sick, or give communion, except on special occasions. Others are available to do these things. So I come and go, a kind of marginal figure in that shell-shocked, lunar, no-person land which is laid claim to by both life and death. *Mors et vita duello conflixere mirando.*

To this hospital, worldly medicine, which bears the false promise of the world, rarely penetrates. (Has anyone ever met a marginal doctor? Psychiatrist? Social worker? They are as rare as marginal priests, or rarer.) But as to our patients, the medicos have already done their damage, served their eviction notices.

The dying drift off, the ship of fools sails majestically over the horizon. Next port of call! We bail, row, weep, swab the decks, change beds, ferry in the newly arrived near dead; and try to keep sane, which means (to keep the nautical metaphor) we steer by the stars, by whatever wit and skill we can summon. And bay at the moon.

This marginal hospital is regarded by the medical profession as a kind of pre-morgue, by the superstitious and drug-ridden in the neighborhood, as a kind of death house. And finally, by the church as an arena of "good works." All such opinions miss the point, which is far removed from common professional activity and attitude.

What really goes on here, as I came to understand, is a test of the Promise, a testing of Christ, whether he might keep his word, whether his spirit might be discovered in such a place. (And as far as I am concerned, whether I might be found in the right place when the Lord comes.)

In the hospital, I am literally disarmed, in a neutral zone, as far as America goes. America, so to speak, cannot go so far, cannot follow. The hospital, for its part, has no interest in proving anything, gaining merit, gaining favor; no cultural fun, games, dodges, feints. Here I am a lesser casualty among casualties, a slower boat on the universal voyage. One trades a blind eye for a firm hand and vice versa, rarely making it among those who are not making it.

The cleric, in the common estimate of church and culture, is a personage, a man (sic) of note. There is, however, another side of a "somebody"; a nobody. I submit that, to be somebody, in the valuable sense of self-knowledge, self-discipline, one must seek to be nobody. The instructions for the journey to the kingdom are quite stringent in this regard.

So I go to the hospital. Unskilled, but perhaps handy, in the way of those who sling hash or wash dishes or wheel carts about in our city. And of course wanting to talk to the dying, to learn from them.

And I recall another, quite different, place when I think of the geography of nobodies. A place where I go and come, crazily, publicly, sociopathically, illegally. To the Pentagon, as formerly to the White House, or, long ago, to the draft board centers. And to the courts rather more frequently, and not as visitor either. Places where people are legally declared marginal, where the marginal fall over the edge. And where, finally, the secular promise (no one need die) is torn up and trampled on. Where, in its stead, a new command is issued: *Obey. Or else.*

––––––––––––––––

In respect to the sane history of humans, the Pentagon is so marginal a project and conception as to be positively hallucinatory.

We must summon a counter-hallucination out of God's storehouse of nightmares in order to remain sane. I have a sense of strange convergence; it is as though one were to place a transparent negative of the hospital over a transparent negative of the Pentagon and find the two exactly coinciding, twin scenes of death. (The hospital image seems well taken; Roosevelt, when the complex was built, promised the nation that the Pentagon would become a hospital after the Second World War.) Instead, in a nightmare of breakaway violence, the place has become a center for the concoction of cancer-for-all, cancer-for-free. I reflect on the fate of our patients, at the hands of techno-medicine men, before they are "dumped" on us. This fate, courtesy of the Pentagon, is now universalized, courtesy of the Pentagon. We have learned a great deal in the last thirty years—from Karen Silkwood, from Paul Jacobs, from Harrisburg. The fate of all of us, that is, is rendered roughly equivalent to the fate of our dying patients. We are to be anesthetized, grotesquely mutilated, experimented on, bombarded with radiation; chemically altered in mind, deceived as to our condition and chances for survival, injected with unknown substances, and so on.

Is this a sci-fi head spin, the dark side of Tolkien, or an accurate delineation of the Pentagonal plan for the last day? *Hiroshima mon amour;* farewell my deadly.

––––––––––––––––

These days, one must admit the possibility, rapidly assuming the form of the probable, that things are all over for the human adventure. I have been battling this sense for some time; I suspect many others do the same. On so thin a margin do we exist, and barely.

Today, few Americans seriously object to my bringing such matters up. What is sad is that we have so waning a confidence that we can turn things around.

For a mad decade, Americans inflicted outrages on others and on the earth; we were profoundly deceived, prattled on about security and a decent future and our children's good chances and an expanding economy. It was all mad as a perfumers' convention on a city dump. The air stank, you held your nose to a perfume bottle and called it reality. Or you took out insurance and called it security. Or you paid your taxes and called it morality.

Another image: It was like a cookout on a battlefield, after the battle. You called it a triumph of *haute cuisine*, you were roasting and eating human parts. (Consult Revelation 19:17.)

———————

If one is marginal to what is sane, he or she might commonly be judged insane. Thus are we often judged by both church and state, which ought to know. But our case might also be put another way. If you are marginal to what is insane, you possibly might be sane. This is how we diagnose ourselves in our communities, having little help except from that old-fashioned handbook called by some "Signs and Portents of Sanity," by others the New Testament.

If one is marginal to what is sane, the meaning of sanity comes up for discussion, inevitably. My working definition is simple; conscientious conduct in the world. Or, more abstractly put, the power of such conduct, sources and skills of such conduct, including soul, inventiveness, daring, tradition and its symbols, community. I want to take sanity out of the hands of nerveless gurus and put it back where it belongs, indeed, where it comes from: the faithful community surviving, resisting at the edge. It takes no great measure of insight to say: Such folk hold the future of the world in their quaking hands.

The judgment might be called immodest in normal times, when the world (turning graciously on its axis, no one claiming more of its fruits, goods, than is their due) could rightly be viewed as gracious partner of a transcendent sense among humans.

Alas, the vehicle is overturned, the times are grossly abnormal, the wheels destructively spin. We had best look anew at the few communities that struggle to keep sane and functional; their claims are rendered modest by immodest times.

Plato said long ago, "The poor person is the one of many needs; the rich person is one of few needs."

Some might be willing today to reclaim a very old wisdom all but buried on some American dump.

Fear of death; you see it in many faces, you hear it on many tongues. People fear the law, they fear jail, they fear the stigma of the outsider. And yet, these may well be ways to sanity. . .

Yet another "marginalizing" is hinted at in Revelation, chapter 13. It goes something like this: You must pay up, a definition of life itself. Then the question arises: In what coin, to whom paid, for what?

If you don't pay Caesar, you pay for it. If you pay Christ,

you pay dear. The choices are not large. I wish with all my crooked heart they were less narrow. In the meantime (which is the only time we have, a twilight, a zone between light and darkness), it is all a gamble, as Pascal said long ago. I prefer to test Christ by refusing Caesar. Let me gamble on him and see what happens.

———————

The analogy of Pentagon and hospital. Each might be considered a shelter for casualties of a death culture. In the hospital, the casualties are simply victims. In the Pentagon, things are visibly (but not necessarily) more complex. The casualties there are arguably both victims and victimizers. In the hospital, patients are finished, they are beyond task or use. In the Pentagon, the casualties keep a certain spurious usefulness; they even inspire a certain awe, are looked on as "top level"—engineers, facilitators, ideologues of the main project and end of the culture, i.e., death. But it must be understood, the generals and technicians and apologues are ethical casualties, by their own devising.

———————

It occurs to me that faith offers no relief from marginality; faith, that is, understood as insight and consequence, follow through, outrage of heart, a shoulder put against the onslaught of death at the door.

Indeed, faith and its symbols, sacraments, its reverent use and celebration of life in the world—these offer no relief. In fact, they intensify the experience of being cast out, rejected, found wanting, declared bizarre, extremist. Faith nudges us toward insecurity, to the edge of accustomed conduct and politesse, that elegant set of rules so often presented as substitute for faith, masking despair and faithlessness. Faith: a clear dialectic in place of a moral smog, a mad pseudo-unity.

We are commonly urged to think of our world as an efficient machine, adamantine, gears smoothly meshing, humming along its tuneless soporific assurance of the abundant life. A good engine in skilled hands, we are assured (in the period B.C., Before Catastrophe). And in the military sector we are told that unscrambled brains pursue, always to our advantage, invincible ends.

Alas, quite the opposite is the case (as the period A.D. reminds us, After Disaster). Mismanagement, fumbling, deceit, cupidity, indifference to the fate of children and the old, the whole a Chaplinesque parody of random, accident-prone fits and starts. But how long a time it takes us, in our bemused trust in the mismanagers, to come to the truth of things! And even then, how much longer before we resist!

Indeed, a case might be made for the following. The world functions least well when Christians are in conformity with it. The world functions less badly when Christians are marginal to it, in resistance against it.

(And yet the world always and inevitably, until the last day, functions badly, if one is to compare its conduct with its own stated goals. Not to speak of comparing it with the ethic of the gospel.)

But our opposition is a gift of truth, as when we say, "How foolish to proclaim that you are democratic when in fact fascist, liberal when oppressive; or to claim you are doing this when, in reality, you are doing that; i.e., educating youth in a humanist tradition, or dispensing justice, or providing medical care or livable housing, or keeping the peace. When, in fact, you are miseducating, multiplying injustice, spreading disease, wasting the earth."

Sometimes we can do more than stand in the shambles and scream. A welfare mother holds up a starving child, poor people sit in at a functionary's home, or release rats in congressional halls. These are gestures of life, powerful and profound and shocking. As is the pouring of blood on the Pentagon. Let the gestures go on! High and useful and on course. . .

. . . Including this one, in this place: a cup of water, in Thy name.